Simply*Circular*™

Edited by Kara Gott Warner

HOUSE of
WHITE
BIRCHES

PUBLISHERS
SINCE 1947

Introduction

Tradition has dictated that using a circular needle is strictly for knitting in the round. If you're ready to bend the rules a bit, and get a little creative with those needles, the ten projects ahead will get you started. You may discover that it's much nicer to "coil" up your needle with your project resting neatly on the cable, rather than having straight needles hazardously pointing out of your knitting bag.

As you work your way through each section, you'll learn a few new ways for working with your circs. *Back & Forth Foundations* introduces you to projects that offer alternatives to working on straight needles. *Basically Bottom Up* and *Totally Top Down* introduce an alluring collection of seamless, in-the-round designs. Then, we'll mix things up a bit with projects worked from side to side in *Off the Cuff*.

When you step out of the static world of straight needles and into the dynamic world of circular knitting, you may wonder why you waited so long to give it a try.

Kara

Kara Gott Warner, editor

Table of Contents

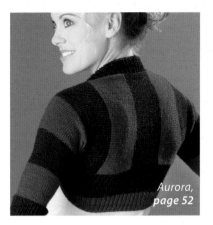

*Aurora,
page 52*

*Calliope Cables,
page 36*

*Thalia Tunic Dress,
page 32*

*Just the
Right Jacket,
page 44*

*Brambles Bag,
page 22*

*Artemis,
page 6*

back & forth *foundations*

When building a house, we always
start with the foundation.

This section is about exploring the circular needle, and learning how useful it can be when working back and forth projects.

When first knitting back and forth on a circular needle, you may wonder how this is possible, considering a circular needle is traditionally intended for working a project in one continuous circle, such as a hat. The trick is to imagine that your circular needle is actually a set of straight needles. After working across a row, simply turn the needle around. The needle in your right hand now becomes the working needle.

Circular Vs. Straight Needles
The reasons are many for opting to use one circular needle over two straight needles. Here are a few to entice you:
- Easy travel—They coil up in your knitting bag, which is a nice feature, especially on a cramped plane. The person in the seat next to you will appreciate not being hit by the ends of your needles!
- You have no dangerous, pointy straight needles protruding out of your knitting bag.
- Your stitches can "stretch" out, giving you the ability to see your project as you go.
- When knitting a large number of stitches, the weight of the knitting is evenly distributed on a circular needle.
- Stitch patterns flow evenly around the garment— they are not interrupted by seams.

Deconstruct To Reconstruct
On the following pages, you'll see many familiar styles, but with a new spin: Instead of working in the traditional way by first working the back of the garment, then the front and finally the sleeves, we suggest doing it all at once on a nice long circular needle. For example, you may work a cardigan starting from the bottom edge, working back and forth from the left front, across the back, ending at the right front edge, all the while keeping your entire project neatly on one needle. Without having to deal with side seams, sewing is kept to a minimum. Working a garment in one piece may sound intimidating, but we promise you'll find it to be an easy and satisfying way to knit. The designs presented are both unique in construction and a breeze to make. You'll find that working on a circular needle brings fluidity to your back and forth projects, creating a natural rhythm to your knitting.

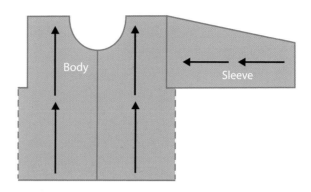

Visual Helpers
Each garment in the book is accompanied by a schematic, helping you to create "checkpoints" as you work through your project. If any adjustments are needed, you can fix these early in the process in order to save the tears later!

Illustrated above, the basic cardigan is worked flat, as one unit. The directional arrows indicate the direction to knit. In this scenario, your cast-on row starts at the bottom. The dotted lines indicate where the garment will be folded when worn. The center line indicates that this garment opens in front. Some important measurements to be aware of include: chest, body length, armhole depth, neck width and depth, shoulder width, sleeve length, sleeve cap height and width.

T!P

HOW TO When choosing a circular needle, it should be short enough so the stitches are not stretched when joined to work in the round. A circular needle can accommodate up to four times the original number of stitches. So if you want to use a different length, take note of the number of stitches to see if your chosen needle can accommodate them.

Artemis

Vests are wardrobe extenders—easy wearing, they mix and match to add style to any outfit.

Design by Jean Clement

Skill Level
◼◼◼◻ INTERMEDIATE

Sizes
Woman's extra-small (small, medium, large, extra-large) Instructions are given for smallest size, with larger sizes in parentheses. When only 1 number is given, it applies to all sizes.

Finished Measurements
Lower Edge: 31¾ (35½, 39, 42¾, 46¼) inches
Waist: 28 (31¼, 34½, 37½, 40¾) inches
Length: 25¾ (26½, 26¾, 28, 29) inches

Materials
- Berroco Lustra (worsted weight; 50% Peruvian wool/50% Tencel Lyocell; 197 yds/100g per hank): 4 (4, 4, 5, 5) hanks Louvre #3107
- Size 6 (4mm) 32-inch circular needle
- Size 7 (4.5mm) 24- and 32-inch circular needles or size needed to obtain gauge
- Cable needle
- Stitch markers
- Stitch holders
- 2 (¾-inch) buttons

4 MEDIUM

Gauge
22 sts and 26 rows = 4 inches/10cm in St st with larger needles.

To save time, take time to check gauge.

Special Abbreviations
Twist 3 Right (T3R): Sl 3 sts to cn, rotate cn ½ turn to right so WS of sts on cn are facing, k3 from cn.

Twist 3 Left (T3L): Sl 3 sts to cn, rotate cn ½ turn to left so WS of sts on cn are facing, k3 from cn.

Pattern Stitch
Body
Rows 1 and 3 (WS): [P3, k1] twice, purl to last 8 sts, [k1, p3] twice.
Row 2 (RS): [K3, p1] twice, knit to last 8 sts, [p1, k3] twice.
Row 4: K3, p1, T3R, p1, knit to last 8 sts, p1, T3L, p1, k3.
Rep Rows 1–4 for pat.

Note: Charts are included for the first and last 8 sts of every row for those preferring to work pat st from a chart.

Special Technique
3-Needle Bind-Off: Hold front and back with RS tog and tips of 2 needles facing in same direction. Using a 3rd needle, *insert RH needle into first st on front needle and then first st on back needle and knit these 2 sts tog; rep from * once more and pass first st on RH needle over 2nd st on RH needle. Continue in same manner until all sts are worked tog. Pull yarn through last st.

Pattern Notes
Circular needles are used to accommodate the large number of stitches; do not join, work back and forth in rows.

This vest is worked flat in 1 piece from the bottom to the top of waist ribbing, and then divided for the armholes; back and each front are worked separately.

Work armhole decreases 2 stitches in from armhole edges, and front neck decreases 9 stitches in from front edges. When decreasing, work a slip, slip, knit (ssk) decrease at beginning of the row and a knit 2 together (k2tog) decrease at end of the row.

Instructions

Body

With larger 32-inch circular needle, cast on 175 (195, 215, 235, 255) sts.

Row 1 (WS): *P1, k1; rep from * to last st, p1.

Row 2 (RS): *K1, p1; rep from * to last st, k1.

Rep Rows 1 and 2 until rib measures 1½ inches, ending with a RS row.

Work Body pat until piece measures 9 (9½, 9½, 10, 10½) inches from cast-on edge, ending with a RS row.

Change to smaller needle for waist rib.

Row 1 (WS): P3,*k1, p1; rep from * to last 4 sts, k1, p3.

Row 2 (RS): K3, *p1, k1; rep from * to last 4 sts, p1, k3.

Rep Rows 1 and 2 until waist rib measures 1¾ (1¾, 1¾, 2¼, 2¼) inches, ending with a RS row.

Change to larger 24-inch circular needle.

Divide Fronts & Back

Next row (WS): [P3, k1] twice, p36 (41, 46, 51, 56), turn. Slip next 87 (97, 107, 117, 127) sts and last 44 (49, 54, 59, 64) sts to separate holders or waste yarn for back and right front—44 (49, 54, 59, 64) sts rem for left front.

Left Front

Continue from Row 2 of Body pat, working pat over 8 sts at neck edge and rem sts in St st. Work 2 rows even.

Neck & armhole shaping

Dec row (armhole, RS): K2, ssk, work as established to end—43 (48, 53, 58, 63) sts.

Work 1 row even.

Dec row (neck): Knit to last 11 sts, k2tog, work in pat to end—42 (47, 52, 57, 62) sts.

Continuing in established pat, dec 1 at armhole edge [every 4 rows] 1 (5, 4, 9, 21) more time(s), then [every 6 rows] 14 (12, 13, 10, 2) times. *At the same time*, dec 1 st at neck edge [every 6 rows] 5 (7, 10, 13, 15) more times, then [every 8 rows] 7 (6, 4, 2, 0) times—15 (17, 21, 23, 24) sts.

Work even in established pat, if necessary, until armhole measures 15 (15¼, 15½, 15¾, 16¼) inches, ending with a RS row. Place sts on holder.

Back

Transfer back sts to working needle. With WS facing, join yarn.

Work 3 rows in St st.

Dec row (RS): K2, ssk, knit to last 4 sts, k2tog, k2—85 (95, 105, 115, 125) sts.

Continue in St st and rep Dec row [every 4 rows] 1 (5, 4, 9, 21) more time(s), then [every 6 rows] 14 (12, 13, 10, 2) times—55 (61, 71, 77, 79) sts.

Work even, if necessary, until armhole measures approx 15 (15¼, 15½, 15¾, 16¼) inches, ending with a WS row.

K15 (17, 21, 23, 24) sts and place on holder or waste yarn for shoulder, bind off 25 (27, 29, 31, 31) back neck sts, k15 (17, 21, 23, 24) sts and place on holder or waste yarn.

Right Front

Transfer right front sts to working needle. With WS facing, join yarn.

Next row (WS): P36 (41, 46, 51, 56), [k1, p3] twice.

Continue from Row 2 of Body pat, working pat over 8 sts at neck edge and rem sts in St st. Work 2 rows even.

Neck & armhole shaping

Dec row (armhole, RS): Work in pat to last 4 sts, k2tog, k2—43 (48, 53, 58, 63) sts.

Work 1 row even.

Dec row (neck): Work as established over first 9 sts, ssk, knit to end—42 (47, 52, 57, 62) sts.

Continuing in established pat, dec 1 at armhole edge [every 4 rows] 1 (5, 4, 9, 21) more time(s), then [every 6 rows] 14 (12, 13, 10, 2) times. *At the same time*, dec 1 st at neck edge [every 6 rows] 5 (7, 10, 13, 15) more times, then [every 8 rows] 7 (6, 4, 2, 0) times—15 (17, 21, 23, 24) sts.

Work even in established pat, if necessary, until armhole measures 15 (15¼, 15½, 15¾, 16¼) inches, ending with a RS row. Place sts on holder.

Finishing

Block to finished measurements.

Join shoulders using 3-Needle Bind-Off.

Armhole band

With smaller needle, pick up and knit 148 (152, 152, 156, 160) sts evenly around armhole. Place marker for beg of rnd and join.

Rnd 1: *K1, p1; rep from * around.

Rnd 2 (dec): Ssk, work in established rib to last 4 sts, k1, k2tog, p1—146 (150, 150, 154, 158) sts.

Rnd 3: K2, work established rib to last 2 sts, k1, p1.

Rnd 4 (dec): Ssk, work in established rib to last 3 sts, k2tog, p1—144 (148, 148, 152, 156) sts.

Rnd 5: Work in established rib around.

Bind off all sts loosely in rib.

Front bands

With RS facing and smaller needle, pick up and knit 122 (128, 130, 136, 142) sts along right front edge, 25 (27, 29, 31, 31) sts across back neck and 122 (128, 130, 136, 142) sts along left front edge—269 (283, 289, 303, 315) sts.

Row 1 (WS): *P1, k1; rep from * to last st, p1.

Work 2 more rows in established rib.

Mark placement for 2 buttons at top and bottom of waist rib, placing markers in purl sts.

Next row: *Work in rib to button marker, yo, k2tog; rep from * once more, work in pat across.

Work 1 row in rib.

Bind off all sts in rib.

Sew buttons opposite buttonholes. •

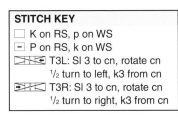

STITCH KEY
- ☐ K on RS, p on WS
- ⊟ P on RS, k on WS
- T3L: Sl 3 to cn, rotate cn ½ turn to left, k3 from cn
- T3R: Sl 3 to cn, rotate cn ½ turn to right, k3 from cn

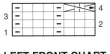

LEFT FRONT CHART

Note: Work at beg of WS rows and end of RS rows

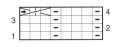

RIGHT FRONT CHART

Note: Work at beg of RS rows and end of WS rows

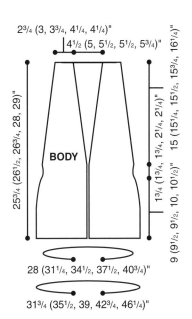

2¾ (3, 3¾, 4¼, 4¼)"

4½ (5, 5½, 5½, 5¾)"

25¾ (26½, 26¾, 28, 29)"

BODY

15 (15¼, 15½, 15¾, 16¼)"

1¾ (1¾, 1¾, 2¼, 2¼)"

1¾ (1¾, 1¾, 2¼, 2¼)"

9 (9½, 9½, 10, 10½)"

28 (31¼, 34½, 37½, 40¾)"

31¾ (35½, 39, 42¾, 46¼)"

Bohemian Rhapsody

Modeled after a man's tailored suit jacket, this piece incorporates edgy details into a classic shape.

Design by Ann Weaver

· ·

Skill Level
◼◼◼◻ EXPERIENCED

Sizes
Woman's extra-small (small, medium, large, extra-large, 2X-large) Instructions are given for smallest size, with larger sizes in parentheses. When only 1 number is given, it applies to all sizes.

Finished Measurements
Chest: 34¾ (39¼, 42¼, 46, 49, 52¾) inches (buttoned)
Length: 21¼ (22½, 23, 23¾, 24, 25) inches

Materials
- Berroco Peruvia (heavy worsted weight; 100% Peruvian highland wool; 174 yds/100g per hank): 5 (5, 6, 7, 7, 7) hanks denim #7142 (MC) and 1 hank azul #7145 (CC)
- Size 9 (5.5mm) 24- and 40-inch circular needle or size needed to obtain gauge
- Stitch holders
- Stitch markers
- 4 (1-inch) buttons

Gauge
16 sts and 22 rows = 4 inches/10cm in St st.

To save time, take time to check gauge.

Special Abbreviations
Knit front and back (kfb): Knit in front and then in back of next st to inc 1 st.

Purl front and back (pfb): Purl in front and then in back of next st to inc 1 st.

Slip, slip, slip, knit (sssk): Slip next 3 sts, 1 at a time, kwise, k3tog-tbl.

Pattern Stitch
Woven (multiple of 3 sts)
Row 1 (RS): Drop MC, pick up CC and, without knitting it, *sl 2 wyif, sl 1 wyib; rep from * across.
Row 2: Carry CC without knitting it, and *sl 1 wyib, sl 2 wyif; rep from * across.
Rows 3–8: Drop CC, pick up MC and work in St st across.
Row 9: Drop MC, pick up CC and, without knitting it, *sl 2 wyib, sl 1 wyif; rep from * across.
Row 10: Carry CC without knitting it, and *sl 1 wyif, sl 2 wyib; rep from * across.
Rows 11–16: Drop CC, pick up MC and work in St st across.
Rep Rows 1–16 for pat, carrying CC loosely along side of work when not in use.

Pattern Notes
This jacket is worked in 1 piece from the bottom up to the armholes; buttonholes, waist and lapel shaping are worked at the same time the body is knit.

After dividing for the armholes, change to shorter needle if you find the longer length uncomfortable to use for shorter rows.

Read the pattern through carefully before beginning; front neck, lapel and armhole shaping occur at the same time.

When working Rows 1, 2, 9 and 10 of the Woven pattern, you will not actually knit with the contrasting-color (CC) yarn; it's woven back and forth between slipped stitches without pulling the contrasting-color yarn.

Markers are placed for the sides of the body and for the lapels; slip markers as you come to them.

Row 4: Purl across.

Continuing in St st, work until body measures 3 (3½, 3½, 3¾, 4, 4) inches, ending with a WS row.

Buttonholes & waist shaping

Dec row 1 (RS): K3, bind off 3 for buttonhole, *knit to 2 sts before marker, ssk, k2tog; rep from * once more, then knit to end—136 (154, 166, 181, 193, 208) sts.

Next row: Purl to buttonhole, cast on 3 sts over bound-off sts, p3—139 (157, 169, 184, 196, 211) sts.

Work even for 4 more rows.

Dec row 2 (RS): *Knit to 2 sts before marker, ssk, k2tog; rep from * once more, then knit to end—135 (153, 165, 180, 192, 207) sts.

Work even for 5 more rows.

Beg Woven pat and work for 2 rows.

Work Row 3 of Woven pat and rep Dec row 1—128 (146, 158, 173, 185, 200) sts.

Work Row 4 of pat and cast on 3 sts over bound-off sts, p3—131 (149, 161, 176, 188, 203) sts.

Work Rows 5–8 of pat even.

Next row (RS): *Work Row 9 of Woven pat to 2 sts before marker, [sl 1 wyib, sl 1 wyif] twice; rep from * once more, then work in pat to end of row.

Next row: *Work Row 10 of Woven pat to 2 sts before marker, [sl 1 wyif, sl 1 wyib] twice; rep from * once more, then work in pat to end of row.

Work Rows 11–16 of pat even.

Next row (RS): *Work Row 1 of Woven pat to 2 sts before marker, [sl 1 wyif, sl 1 wyib] twice; rep from * once more, then work in pat to end of row.

Next row: *Work Row 2 of Woven pat to 2 sts before marker, [sl 1 wyib, sl 1 wyif] twice; rep from * once more, then work in pat to end of row.

Inc row 1 (RS): K3, bind off 3 for buttonhole, *knit to 1 st before marker, [kfb] twice; rep from * once more, then knit to end—132 (150, 162, 177, 189, 204) sts.

Next row: Purl to buttonhole, cast on 3 sts over bound-off sts, p3—135 (153, 165, 180, 192, 207) sts.

Work Rows 5–10 of pat even.

Inc row 2: *Knit to 1 st before marker, [kfb] twice; rep from * once more, then knit to end—139 (157, 169, 184, 196, 211) sts.

Instructions

Body

With CC and longer needle, cast on 38 (44, 47, 50, 53, 56) sts for right front, place marker, cast on 67 (73, 79, 88, 94, 103) sts for back, place marker, cast on 38 (44, 47, 50, 53, 56) sts for left front—143 (161, 173, 188, 200, 215) sts.

Row 1 (RS): Knit across, cut yarn.

Row 2: Join MC and knit across.

Row 3: *K1, p1; rep from * across.

Work Rows 12–16 of pat even.

Next row (RS): *Work Row 1 of Woven pat to 1 st before marker, sl 1 wyif, sl 1 wyib; rep from * once more, then work in pat to end of row.

Next row: *Work Row 2 of Woven pat to 1 st before marker, sl 1 wyib, sl 1 wyif; rep from * once more, then work in pat to end of row. Cut CC and continue in St st with MC only.

Rep Inc row 1—140 (158, 170, 185, 197, 212) sts.

Next row: Purl to buttonhole, cast on 3 sts over bound-off sts, p3—143 (161, 173, 188, 200, 215) sts.

Work even in St st until body measures 10 (10½, 10½, 10¾, 11, 11) inches from cast-on.

Shape lapels & front neck
Row 1 (set-up, WS): Kfb, place lapel marker, purl to last st, place lapel marker, kfb—145 (163, 175, 190, 202, 217) sts with 2 lapel sts and 37 (43, 46, 49, 52, 55) front sts each side.

Row 2 (inc lapel/dec front neck, RS): Pfb, purl to lapel marker, yo, k3tog, knit to 3 sts before lapel marker, sssk, yo, purl to last 2 sts, pfb, p1— 3 lapel sts and 36 (42, 45, 48, 51, 54) front sts each side.

Row 3 and all WS rows: Knit to first lapel marker, purl to 2nd lapel marker, knit to end.

Continue to inc for lapels [every RS row] 6 (6, 6, 7, 7, 7) more times, then [every 4 rows] 4 (5, 5, 5, 5, 6) times, and *at the same time*, dec at neck edges [every RS row] 4 (10, 8, 5, 5, 2) more times, and [every 4 rows] 12 (10, 12, 14, 14, 17) times. On every RS row with no neck dec, work between lapel markers as follows: yo, k2tog, knit to 2 sts before lapel marker, ssk, yo.

At the same time, when body measures 13¼ (14¼, 14¼, 14½, 14¾, 15¼) inches from cast-on edge, end with a RS row.

Divide for armholes
Next row (WS): *Work to 4 (4, 4, 5, 5, 5) sts before side marker, bind off next 8 (8, 8, 10, 10, 10) sts for armhole; rep from * once, then work to end of row. Place 59 (65, 71, 78, 84, 93) back sts and left front sts on holders or waste yarn.

Right Front
Continuing rem lapel incs and neck decs as established, bind off at beg of WS rows [2 (3, 2, 3, 3, 3) sts] once. Dec at armhole edge [1 st] 2 (3, 3, 4, 5, 7) times.

When lapel shaping is complete, continue neck decs until front measures approx 5¼ (5¾, 5¾, 6¼, 6¼, 6¾) inches from beg of lapel, ending with a WS row.

Upper lapel
Next row (RS): Continuing rem front neck shaping as established, bind off 7 (8, 8, 9, 9, 10) lapel sts pwise—5 lapel sts rem.

Next row and all rem WS rows: Work even.

Inc row (RS): Pfb, work as established to end of row—6 lapel sts.

Continue to inc for upper lapel [every RS row] 6 (7, 7, 9, 9, 10) more times—12 (13, 13, 15, 15, 16) lapel sts and 13 (13, 17, 18, 20, 20) front sts when all shaping is complete.

Work even until armhole measures 7¼ (7½, 8, 8½, 8½, 9) inches, ending with a RS row.

Place 12 (13, 13, 15, 15, 16) lapel sts on holder.

Shape shoulders
Bind off at beg of WS rows, [5 (5, 6, 6, 7, 7) sts] once, [4 (4, 6, 6, 7, 7) sts] once, then [4 (4, 5, 6, 6, 6) sts] once.

Left Front
Place sts from holder on shorter needle, join yarn with RS facing.

Continuing rem lapel incs and neck decs as established, bind off at beg of RS rows, [2 (3, 2, 3, 3, 3) sts] once. Dec at armhole [1 st] 2 (3, 3, 4, 5, 7) times.

When lapel shaping is complete, continue neck decs until front measures approx 5¼ (5¾, 5¾, 6¼, 6¼, 6¾) inches from beg of lapel, ending with a RS row.

Upper lapel
Next row (WS): Continuing rem front neck shaping as established, bind off 7 (8, 8, 9, 9, 10) lapel sts kwise—5 lapel sts rem.

Inc row (RS): Work as established to last 2 sts, pfb, p1—6 lapel sts.

Next row and all rem WS rows: Work even.

Continue to inc for upper lapel [every RS row] 6 (7, 7, 9, 9, 10) more times—12 (13, 13, 15, 15, 16) lapel sts and 13 (13, 17, 18, 20, 20) front sts when all shaping is complete.

Work even until armhole measures 7¼ (7½, 8, 8½, 8½, 9) inches, ending with a WS row.

Place 12 (13, 13, 15, 15, 16) lapel sts on holder.

Shape shoulders
Bind off at beg of RS rows, [5 (5, 6, 6, 7, 7) sts] once, [4 (4, 6, 6, 7, 7) sts] once, then [4 (4, 5, 6, 6, 6) sts] once.

Back
Place sts from holder on short needle, join yarn with RS facing.

Bind off [2 (3, 2, 3, 3, 3) sts] at beg of next 2 rows—55 (59, 67, 72, 78, 87) sts.

Dec row (RS): Sl 1, ssk, knit to last 3 sts, k2tog, k1—53 (57, 65, 70, 76, 85) sts.

Rep Dec row [every RS row] 1 (2, 2, 3, 4, 6) more time(s)—51 (53, 61, 64, 68, 73) sts.

Work even until armhole measures approx 7¼ (7½, 8, 8½, 8½, 9) inches, ending with a WS row.

Shape neck & shoulders
Row 1 (RS): K15 (15, 19, 20, 22, 22) sts, join a 2nd ball of yarn and bind off next 21 (23, 23, 24, 24, 29) sts, knit to end.

Work both sides at once with separate balls of yarn.

Row 2: Bind off 5 (5, 6, 6, 7, 7) shoulder sts, purl across; other side, purl across.

Row 3: Bind off 5 (5, 6, 6, 7, 7) shoulder sts, knit to last 3 sts, k2tog, k1; other side, k1, ssk, knit to end.

Row 4: Bind off 4 (4, 6, 6, 7, 7) shoulder sts, purl across; other side, purl across.

Row 5: Bind off 4 (4, 6, 6, 7, 7) shoulder sts, knit to last 3 sts, k2tog, k1; other side, k1, ssk, knit to end.

Row 6: Bind off rem left shoulder sts; other side, purl across.

Bind off rem right shoulder sts.

Sleeves
With shorter needle and CC, cast on 45 (48, 48, 51, 51, 54) sts.

Row 1 (RS): Knit across, cut yarn.

Row 2: Join MC and knit across.

Row 3: *K1, p1; rep from * across.

Row 4: Purl across.

Continuing in St st, work until sleeve measures 7¼ (7½, 7½, 7¾, 7¾, 8) inches, ending with a WS row.

Work [Rows 1–16] of Woven pat, then work [Rows 1–10] once more.

Inc row (RS): With MC, k1, kfb, knit to last 2 sts, kfb, k1—47 (50, 50, 53, 53, 56) sts.

Continue in established pat until 5 stripes have been worked, then continue in St st, and *at the same time*, rep Inc row [every 12 rows] 3 more times—53 (56, 56, 59, 59, 62) sts.

Work even until sleeve measures 17½ (18, 18, 18½, 18½, 19) inches, ending with a WS row.

Shape cap
Bind off 4 (4, 4, 5, 5, 5) sts at beg of the next 2 rows, then 2 (3, 2, 3, 3, 3) sts at beg of the following 2 rows—41 (42, 44, 43, 43, 46) sts.

Work 2 rows even.

Dec row (RS): K1, ssk, work to last 3 sts, k2tog, k1—39 (40, 42, 41, 41, 44) sts.

Rep Dec row [every RS row] 6 (4, 4, 0, 0, 0) more times, then [every 4 rows] 1 (3, 3, 6, 6, 7) time(s)—25 (26, 28, 29, 29, 30) sts.

Bind off 3 sts at beg of the next 4 rows—13 (14, 16, 17, 17, 18) sts.

Bind off rem sts.

Finishing
Block pieces to finished measurements.

Sew shoulder seams.

Back collar
Place 12 (13, 13, 15, 15, 16) right front lapel sts on short needle; join yarn with RS facing.

Work even in St st until piece reaches approx 1 inch past center of back neck. Place sts on holder.

Rep for left front lapel sts.

Graft back collar sts tog using Kitchener st (see page 59).

Using MC, sew back collar to back neck edge, easing extra collar length into the neck.

Right front edging
With RS facing and CC, beg at lower edge, pick up and knit approx 4 sts for every 5 rows along front edge to beg of lapel shaping.

Knit 1 row.

Bind off very loosely. Cut yarn.

Left front edging

With RS facing and CC, beg at bottom of lapel shaping, pick up and knit approx 4 sts for every 5 rows along front edge to bottom edge.

Knit 1 row.

Bind off very loosely. Cut yarn.

Lapels & collar edging

Note: Edging for ends of lapels and collar, and long edge of collar are worked separately, picking sts up along the knit side for each section.

With knit side of lapel facing and CC, beg at bottom of left lapel shaping, pick up and knit approx 5 sts for every 6 rows along edge of left lapel.

Knit 1 row.

Bind off very loosely, leaving last st on needle.

Pick up and knit 1 st in each st along top edge of left lapel, ending at corner notch.

Knit 1 row.

Bind off loosely, leaving last st on needle.

Pick up and knit approx 5 sts for every 6 rows along edge of upper left lapel, approx 4 sts for every 5 rows along back collar, and 5 sts for every 6 rows along upper right lapel, ending at corner of notch.

Knit 1 row.

Bind off loosely, leaving last st on needle.

Pick up and knit 1 st in each st along top edge of right lapel, ending at point.

Knit 1 row.

Bind off loosely, leaving last st on needle.

Pick up and knit approx 5 sts for every 6 rows along edge of right lapel, ending at beg of lapel shaping.

Knit 1 row.

Bind off all sts loosely.

Sew sleeve seams. Set in sleeves.

Sew buttons to left front opposite buttonholes.

Block back neck, armhole and sleeve seams. ●

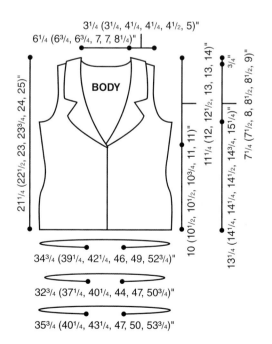

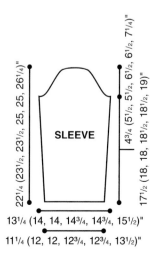

With our foundation in place, it's time to move into new territory.

basically bottom up

In many respects, working a seamless garment is easier than flat back and forth knitting. One obvious reason is the lack of sewing involved. If sewing isn't your forte, or you don't feel confident in your finishing abilities, then in-the-round knitting is the perfect solution. How many unfinished sweaters do you have in your closet?

Gauge

Don't be tempted to jump right in without checking your gauge! It's a critical component to successful garment construction and should never be overlooked. When it comes to knitting in the round, gauge is not the same as when knitting a flat garment. The reason for this is that a knitter's tension is usually different when purling than when knitting. Also, knitting circularly can change the yardage consumed for a given project.

Make the Swatch

The bottom-up method is usually the simplest because unlike top-down construction which involves neck shaping at the very beginning, bottom-up construction starts at the bottom of the garment, which usually requires very little, if any, shaping. The best way to visualize your garment is to imagine a cylindrical tube. Knitting in the round is a seamless method of working a circular garment like a pullover. But before we build upon the concept of the tube, it's important to understand the fundamentals of casting on.

Casting Onto a Circular Needle

Step 1: After casting on the required number of stitches, place your work down on a flat surface, making sure the cast-on edge faces the center as indicated by the arrows. This will ensure that your stitches do not twist around the needle.

Step 2: Join the work by placing a marker on the right-hand needle so that you'll remember the location of the beginning of the round. Then, knit into the first stitch that you cast on, creating a "ring."

Working on Double-Point Needles

Most projects in this book are worked on circular needles for comfort and ease, but in some cases, projects may call for double-point

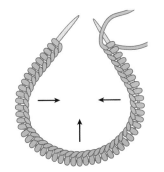

needles for the following reasons: either you're working small circumference pieces, or you've decreased several stitches (which creates a smaller circumference), or your circular needle is too long to accommodate your stitches. Refer to page 60 for a detailed explanation for working with double-point needles.

Working "The Tube"

Directional arrows indicate that this piece is knitted from the bottom up to the armhole, with the sleeves knitted in the round, and then joined to the body. All the pieces are then joined and knit together to form the yoke, ending with the neck.

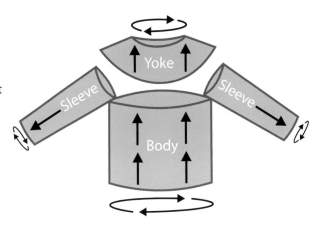

T!P

HOW TO *When working your first round, to keep your stitches from twisting around the needle, try using several clothespins to hold the stitches in place, removing them as you work; or, work one row before joining into a circle. When you're done, sew the small opening closed.*

Selene

Perfectly understated, this casual design is the right choice for any occasion.

Design by Andra Knight-Bowman

Skill Level
■■□□ EASY

Sizes
Woman's extra-small (small, medium, large, extra-large) Instructions are given for smallest size, with larger sizes in parentheses. When only 1 number is given, it applies to all sizes.

Finished Measurements
Chest: 30 (33¼, 36¾, 40, 43¼) inches
Length: 20 (21, 22, 23, 24½) inches

Materials
- Rowan Lima (worsted weight; 84% baby alpaca/8% merino wool/ 8% nylon; 109 yds/50g per ball): 5 (6, 7, 7, 8) balls Machu Picchu #885
- Size 7 (4.5mm) 16- and 32-inch circular needles or size needed to obtain gauge
- Stitch markers, 1 in CC for beg of rnd
- Stitch holders

4 MEDIUM

Gauge
24 sts and 33 rnds = 4 inches/10cm in St st.

To save time, take time to check gauge.

Special Abbreviation
Make 1 (M1): Insert LH needle from front to back under the horizontal thread between the last st worked and next st on LH needle; k1-tbl.

Pattern Stitch
Garter St (worked in the rnd)
Rnd 1: Purl around.
Rnd 2: Knit around.
Rep [Rnds 1 and 2] for pat.

Special Technique
3-Needle Bind-Off: Hold front and back with RS tog and tips of 2 needles facing in same direction. Using a 3rd needle, *insert RH needle into first st on front needle and then first st on back needle and knit these 2 sts tog; rep from * once more and pass first st on RH needle over 2nd st on RH needle. Continue in same manner until all sts are worked tog. Pull yarn through last st.

Pattern Notes
This shell is worked from the bottom up. The lower garter stitch borders are worked first and joined, after which the body is knit in the round to underarms. Front and back are worked separately from armhole to shoulder.

A wide garter stitch collar is worked after garment is complete.

Slip first stitch of all rows purlwise with yarn in front; bring yarn to back and continue to work row.

Instructions

Bottom Borders
Cast on 90 (100, 110, 120, 130) sts.

Rows 1–10: Sl 1, knit to end.

Row 11 (WS): Sl 1, k5, purl to last 6 sts, knit to end.

Row 12 (RS): Sl 1, knit to end.

Rep [Rows 11 and 12] 6 times more; cut yarn and leave sts on needle.

Rep for 2nd border; after last row, do not turn, and do not cut yarn.

Body
Rnd 1: Place marker for beg of rnd and knit across first set of border sts; place marker for side, and knit across 2nd set of border sts—180 (200, 220, 240, 260) sts.

Work even in St st in rnds until piece measures 12½ (13, 13½, 14, 15) inches from cast-on edge.

Divide for Back & Front

Next row (RS): Sl 1, k5, ssk, knit to 8 sts before side marker, k2tog, k6, turn; place rem sts on holder or waste yarn for front—88 (98, 108, 118, 128) back sts.

Back

Row 1 (WS): Sl 1, k5, purl to last 6 sts, k6.

Row 2 (RS): Sl 1, k5, ssk, knit to last 8 sts, k2tog, k6—86 (96, 106, 116, 126) sts.

Rep [Rows 1 and 2] 11 (11, 11, 12, 16) more times—64 (74, 84, 92, 94) sts.

Work even until armhole measures 7½ (8, 8½, 9, 9½) inches.

Place first 17 (20, 23, 26, 26) shoulder sts, 30 (34, 38, 40, 42) back neck sts, and last 17 (20, 23, 26, 26) shoulder sts on separate holders or waste yarn.

Front

Work as for back until armholes measure 5½ (6, 6½, 7, 7½) inches, ending with a WS row.

Shape neck

Next row (RS): Sl 1, k21 (24, 27, 30, 30), place center 20 (24, 28, 30, 32) sts on holder or waste yarn, join a 2nd ball of yarn, k22 (25, 28, 31, 31).

Dec row (WS): Working both sides at once with separate balls of yarn, work to 3 sts before neck edge, ssp, p1; p1, p2tog, work to end—21 (24, 27, 30, 30) sts each side.

Dec row (RS): Work to 3 sts before neck edge, k2tog, k1; k1, ssk, work to end—20 (23, 26, 29, 29) sts each side.

Continue to dec at each neck edge [every row] 3 more times—17 (20, 23, 26, 26) sts each side.

Work even until armhole measures 7½ (8, 8½, 9, 9½) inches.

Finishing

Place left back shoulder sts on needle. Join shoulder using 3-Needle Bind-Off.

Rep for right shoulder.

Block to finished measurements.

Collar

With RS facing and 16-inch circular needle, beg at left shoulder, pick up and knit 47 (50, 53, 58, 63) sts along front neck, then knit sts from back holder—77 (84, 91, 98, 105) sts.

Place marker for beg of rnd and join.

Work in garter st until collar measures 2 inches, beg and end with a purl rnd.

Inc rnd: *K7, M1; rep from * around—88 (96, 104, 112, 120) sts.

Simply Circular

Continue in garter st for 1 inch, ending with a purl rnd.

Inc rnd: *K8, M1; rep from * around—99 (108, 117, 126, 135) sts.

Continue in garter st for 1 inch, ending with a purl rnd.

Inc rnd: *K9, M1; rep from * around—110 (120, 130, 140, 150) sts.

Continue in garter st for 1 inch, ending with a purl rnd.

Bind off all sts loosely kwise. ●

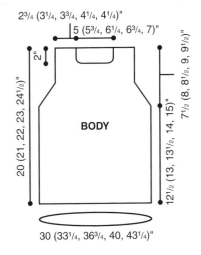

2¾ (3¼, 3¾, 4¼, 4¼)"

5 (5¾, 6¼, 6¾, 7)"

2"

20 (21, 22, 23, 24½)"

BODY

7½ (8, 8½, 9, 9½)"

12½ (13, 13½, 14, 15)"

30 (33¼, 36¾, 40, 43¼)"

Brambles Bag

Except for its rectangular shape, there is nothing traditional about the variegated yarn, bramble stitch stripes and knit-in lining, all of which make this shoulder bag stand out from the crowd.

Design by Talitha Kuomi

Skill Level

■■■□ INTERMEDIATE

Finished Size
Approx 14 inches high x 10½ inches wide x 2 inches deep, blocked.

Materials

- Plymouth Yarn Co. Boku (worsted weight; 95% wool/5% silk; 99 yds/50g per ball): 9 balls red/orange/brown/blue #9
- Size 6 (4mm) 24-inch circular and double-point needles (set of 5) or size needed to obtain gauge
- Stitch markers
- Locking stitch markers
- Stitch holder

Gauge
21 sts and 30 rnds/rows = 4 inches/10cm in St st and Bramble St pat (blocked).

20 sts and 30 rnds = 4 inches/10 cm in St st (blocked).

To save time, take time to check gauge.

Special Abbreviations
N1, N2, N3, N4: Needle 1, Needle 2, Needle 3, Needle 4.

Pattern Stitches
Bramble St (multiple of 4 sts, worked in rnds)
Rnds 1 and 3: Purl around.
Rnd 2: *(P1, k1, p1) all in the same st, k3tog; rep from * around.
Rnd 4: *K3tog, (p1, k1, p1) all in the same st; rep from * around.
Rep Rnds 1–4 for pat.

Bramble St (multiple of 4 sts, worked in rows)
Rows 1 and 3 (RS): Purl across.
Row 2: *(K1, p1, k1) all in the same st, p3tog; rep from * across.
Row 4: *P3tog, (k1, p1, k1) all in the same st; rep from * across.
Rep Rows 1–4 for pat.

Pattern Notes
The outer bag is worked in the round from the bottom. After the outer flap is complete, the flap and bag linings are worked back to the bottom.

Purl ridges are used as fold lines so the top-flap lining and inner bag can easily be folded to the inside of the bag.

Instructions

Outer Bag
With circular needle, cast on 132 sts. Place marker for beg of rnd and join, taking care not to twist sts.

Work in Bramble St pat for 28 rnds.

*Work in St st for 13 rnds, then work in Bramble St pat for 12 rnds; rep from * twice more. Work in St st for 13 rnds.

Next rnd: P76 and slip to holder or waste yarn for front, purl to end—56 sts rem.

Outer Flap
Work back and forth over rem sts.

Continuing from Row 2, work in Bramble St pat for 11 rows.

*Work 12 rows of St st, then work 12 rows of Bramble St pat; rep from * once more.

Next row (RS): Purl across for fold line for top of flap.

Flap Lining

Dec row: P3, [p2tog, p5] 7 times, p2tog, p2—48 sts.

Continue in St st until top flap measures approx 8 inches from Dec row, ending with a WS row.

Bag Lining

Transfer front sts from holder to main needle.

With RS facing, *k3, [k2tog, k5] 10 times, k3; rep from * across front sts, knit flap sts—114 sts.

Place marker for beg of rnd and join.

Continue in St st until inner bag measures approx 14½ inches from fold line for inner bag.

Bind off 66 sts, then knit to end—48 sts.

Lining bottom

Continue back and forth in St st over rem sts for 1¾ inches.

Bind off all sts loosely.

Strap

With dpn, beg to left of top flap, pick up and knit 16 sts below the purl row along the top outside edge of bag, turn bag with lining facing, pick up and knit 12 sts below the purl row along lining—28 sts.

Divide sts with 8 sts each on N1 and N2 for top of strap, and 6 sts each on N3 and N4 for bottom of strap. Place marker for beg of rnd and join.

Rnds 1–12: N1 and N2: work Bramble St pat across; N3 and N4: knit across.

Rnds 13–25: Work in St st over all sts for 13 rnds.

Rep Rnds 1–25 until strap measures approx 24 inches, ending with Rnd 12.

Bind off all sts loosely.

Finishing

Fold top flap at fold line. Sew flap and lining tog along the side edges.

Block to measurements.

Sew shoulder strap to top edge of bag, to the right of top flap, corresponding position of beg of strap.

Turn bag with WS facing. Lay bag flat with flap centered and straps at each side. Whipstitch cast-on edge closed.

Place locking markers along bottom edge and sides of bag, each approx 1½ inches from both bottom corners (see Figure 1). Open out 1 corner and fold with RS tog, and so that bottom seam and side of bag are tog; markers should meet (see Figure 2). Mark a line across corner and perpendicular to bottom seam. Sew across corner at marked line.

Rep with other corner.

Turn bag with RS facing.

Sew lining bottom to bound-off edge of lining. Place lining inside bag. ●

FIGURE 1

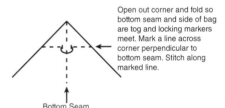

Open out corner and fold so bottom seam and side of bag are tog and locking markers meet. Mark a line across corner perpendicular to bottom seam. Stitch along marked line.

Bottom Seam

FIGURE 2

Calypso Capelet

Based on a traditional Orenburg shawl technique, this cowl is worked in garter-stitch lace. The border is worked in rows and sewn into a circle. The rest of the shaped cowl is knit in the round, featuring three different spring-inspired motifs.

Design by Faiṅa Goberstein

Skill Level
◼◼◼▢ INTERMEDIATE

Size
1 size fits most

Finished Measurements
Bottom circumference: 51 inches, blocked
Depth: 12 inches, blocked

Materials
- Louet North America Mooi (lace weight; 70% rayon from bamboo/15% bison/15% cashmere; 350 yds/50g per skein): 2 skeins amethyst #03
- Size 1 (2.25mm) double-point or straight needles
- Size 2 (2.75mm) 24-inch circular needle or size needed to obtain gauge
- Stitch markers

Gauge
28 sts and 56 rnds = 4 inches/10cm in garter st with larger needle, blocked.

To save time, take time to check gauge.

Pattern Stitches
Lace Border (10-st pat, beg with 9 sts, inc to 14 sts, then dec to 10 sts)
Row 1 (WS): Knit across.
Row 2 (RS): Sl 1 wyif, k2, yo, k6—10 sts.
Rows 3, 5, 7, 9 and 11: Sl 1 wyif, knit across.
Row 4: Sl 1 wyif, k2, yo, k7—11 sts.
Row 6: Sl 1 wyif, k2, yo, k8—12 sts.
Row 8: Sl 1 wyif, k2, yo, k3, yo, k2tog, k4—13 sts.
Row 10: Sl 1 wyif, k2, yo, k3, [yo, k2tog] twice, k3—14 sts.

Row 12: Sl 1 wyif, k3, yo, k2tog, k2, yo, k2tog, k4.
Row 13: Sl 1 wyif, k11, k2tog—13 sts.
Row 14: Sl 1 wyif, k3, yo, k2tog, k7.
Row 15: Sl 1 wyif, k10, k2tog—12 sts.
Row 16: Sl 1 wyif, k3, yo, k2tog, k6.
Row 17: Sl 1 wyif, k9, k2tog—11 sts.
Row 18: Sl 1 wyif, k3, yo, k2tog, k5.
Row 19: Sl 1 wyif, k8, k2tog—10 sts.
Rows 20–34: Rep Rows 4–18.
Rep Rows 19–34 for pat.

Fallen Trees (multiple of 20 sts)
Rnd 1: *Yo, k2tog, k18; rep from * around.
Rnd 2 and all even-numbered rnds: Purl around.
Rnd 3: *[Yo, k2tog] twice, k16; rep from * around.
Rnd 5: *[Yo, k2tog] 3 times, k14; rep from * around.
Rnd 7: *[Yo, k2tog] 4 times, k12; rep from * around.
Rnd 9: *[Yo, k2tog] 5 times, k10; rep from * around.
Rnd 11: *[Yo, k2tog] 6 times, k8; rep from * around.
Rnd 13: Rep Rnd 9.
Rnd 15: Rep Rnd 7.
Rnd 17: Rep Rnd 5.
Rnd 19: Rep Rnd 3.
Rnd 21: Rep Rnd 1.

Strawberries (multiple of 13 sts)
Rnd 1: *K2, [yo, k2tog] twice, k7; rep from * around.
Rnds 2 and 4: Purl around.
Rnd 3: *K2tog, yo, k3, yo, k2tog, k6; rep from * around.
Rnd 5: *K2, yo, k3tog, yo, k8; rep from * around.

Mouse Prints (multiple of 9 sts, dec to 8 on first rnd)
Rnd 1: *K1, yo, k2tog, k4, k2tog; rep from * around.
Rnds 2 and 4: Purl around.
Rnd 3: *[Yo, k2tog] twice, k4; rep from * around.
Rnd 5: *K1, yo, k2tog, k5; rep from * around.

Garter St (worked in the rnd)
Rnd 1: Purl around.
Rnd 2: Knit around.
Rep Rnds 1 and 2 for pat.

Special Technique
3-Needle Bind-Off: Hold ends of Border with RS tog and tips of 2 needles facing in same direction. Using a 3rd needle, *insert RH needle into first st on front needle and then first st on back needle and knit these 2 sts tog; rep from * once more and pass first st on RH needle over 2nd st on RH needle. Continue in same manner until indicated number of sts are worked.

Pattern Notes
Always begin garter stitch with a purl round, unless otherwise instructed.

Charts are provided for those preferring to work from a chart.

To make it easier to work the lace patterns, place markers at end of each stitch repeat around.

The gauge after blocking will be very different than before blocking; make sure to block the gauge swatch to ensure accurate sizing.

Instructions

Border
With smaller needles and waste yarn, cast on 9 sts. Join working yarn.

Work [Rows 1–34] of Lace Border pat, then rep [Rows 19–34] 26 more times—28 peaks.

Remove waste yarn from cast-on and place 9 sts on needle.

With RS tog, beg at straight edge and join ends using 3-Needle Bind-Off over first 9 sts, bind off rem st.

Cowl
With larger needle and RS facing and working through back loop of slipped selvage st only, pick up sts along straight edge of border as follows:

*[Pick up and knit 4 sts, yo, pick up and knit 1 st] 3 times, pick up and knit 2 sts, yo, pick up and knit 1 st; rep from * 11 more times, [pick up and knit 4 sts, yo, pick up and knit 1 st] 2 times, pick up and knit 2 sts, yo, pick up and knit 1 st—280 sts. Place marker for beg of rnd and join.
Work in garter st for 5 rnds, ending with a purl rnd.

Next rnd: *Yo, k2tog; rep from * around.

Continue in garter st for 7 rnds, ending with a purl rnd.

Work Rnds 1–21 of Fallen Trees pat.

Continue in garter st for 7 rnds, ending with a purl rnd.

Next rnd: *Yo, k2tog; rep from * around.

Continue in garter st for 7 rnds, ending with a purl rnd.

Next rnd: *Yo, k2tog; rep from * around.

Continue in garter st for 2 rnds.

Dec rnd: *P2tog, p12; rep from * around—260 sts.

Continue in garter st for 2 rnds.

Work Rnds 1–5 of Strawberries pat.

Continue in garter st for 4 rnds, ending with a knit rnd.

Dec rnd: *P2tog, p11; rep from * around—240 sts.

Next rnd: *Yo, k2tog; rep from * around.

Continue in garter st for 6 rnds, ending with a knit rnd.

Dec rnd: *P2tog, p10; rep from * around—220 sts.

Continue in garter st for 7 rnds, ending with a knit rnd.

Dec rnd: *P2tog, p9; rep from * around—200 sts.

Next rnd: *Yo, k2tog; rep from * around.

Continue in garter st for 6 rnds, ending with a knit rnd.

Dec rnd: *P2tog, p8; rep from * around—180 sts.

Work Rnds 1–5 of Mouse Prints pat—160 sts.

Continue in garter st for 6 rnds, ending with a knit rnd.

Dec rnd: *P2tog, p6; rep from * around—140 sts.

Next rnd: *Yo, k2tog; rep from * around.

Continue in garter st for 6 rnds, ending with a knit rnd.

Dec rnd: *P2tog, p5; rep from * around—120 sts.

Continue in garter st for 2 rnds.

Knit 20 rnds.

Bind off all sts loosely.

Finishing
Weave in ends.

Block to finished measurements, placing pins in each of the 28 peaks to shape. ●

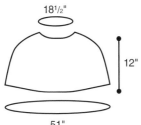

18½"

12"

51"

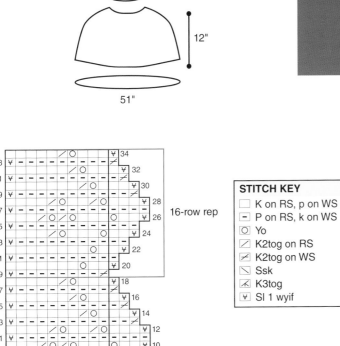

STRAWBERRIES CHART

13-st rep

STITCH KEY
- ☐ K on RS, p on WS
- – P on RS, k on WS
- ○ Yo
- ╱ K2tog on RS
- ╱ K2tog on WS
- ╲ Ssk
- ✕ K3tog
- ¥ Sl 1 wyif

LACE BORDER CHART

16-row rep

MOUSE PRINTS CHART

8-st rep

FALLEN TREES CHART

20-st rep

totally top down

Now that you have a good grounding in circular knitting, working from the top down has some great advantages.

Since you begin from the neck opening, your most crucial shaping sections, such as armholes and bust, are worked first, long before the waist shaping. This saves you from the possible nightmare of knitting flat pieces and seaming them together, only to realize that your waist shaping was incorrect! With the top-down method, your shaping elements have been determined, allowing some "creative license" to lengthen your sweater or make it slightly shorter, if preferred.

Engineered Elements

As stressed in previous chapters, the schematic is always positioned the way the garment will be worked, with top-down projects, you will notice that the schematic is positioned upside down, with the neck as the cast-on round.

Shown in the illustration at the right, after casting on for the back neck, you will work the raglan shaping for the fronts, back and sleeves at the same time that you are shaping the V-neck; since the V-neck is "open," you will be working back and forth. After the V-neck shaping is complete, you will join the two ends of the piece at the front neck and continue by working in the round. When the raglan shaping is done, you will bind off the sleeve stitches, and then continue working the body, shaping the waist before binding off.

Shaping Elements

Circular knitting takes on a 3-dimensional form, unlike static flat, back-and-forth knitting. There are many ways to work a circular design because of its "sculptural" aspects. For example, fitted sections of the waist and bust can be worked in a simpler way than one would do with a project knitted flat. With top-down knitting, you can literally try the piece on while you work.

Here are some common shapes found in circular knitting that can "molded" into different forms:

- **Straight, unshaped tubes:** These may become neck warmers, tote bags, fingerless gloves or the body of a pullover.

- **Shaped tubes:** These may become sleeves, hats and waist-shaping sections on the body of a pullover.

- **Cones:** A very shallow cone may become the yoke of a sweater, worked with proportionally spaced decrease rounds.

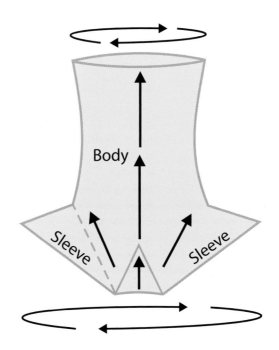

- **Domes:** These are commonly found in hats, where shaping sections are evenly spaced, until most of the stitches are severely decreased to the top.

HOW TO To make a neater join, cast on one more stitch than called for in your pattern onto your circular needle, or double-point needles, and then slip the first stitch from the left-hand needle onto the right-hand needle. Lift the next stitch on the right-hand needle and place it over the slipped stitch. This creates a smooth cast-on edge.

Thalia Tunic Dress

The top-down dress is one of those projects where you have very little sewing to do. It's worked circularly, beginning at the neck and continuing down to the hem, becoming a comfortable, easy-to-wear dress. The raglan armholes and skirt gores are created using fully fashioned increases, and waist shaping is achieved by switching to a cable and rib pattern.

Design by Mihaela Manitu

Skill Level

■■■□ EXPERIENCED

Sizes

Woman's extra-small (small, medium, large, extra-large) Instructions are given for smallest size, with larger sizes in parentheses. When only 1 number is given, it applies to all sizes.

Finished Measurements

Chest: 32 (35½, 40, 44½, 48) inches
Length: 33¼ (34½, 35¼, 36¼, 37½) inches

Materials

- Berroco Weekend (worsted weight; 75% acrylic/25% Peruvian cotton; 205 yds/100g per hank): 4 (4, 5, 5, 5) hanks oats #5903 (MC), 2 hanks damask #5933 (A), 1 (2, 2, 2, 2) hank(s) mouse #5907 (B) and 1 hank raisin #5906 (C)
- Size 7 (4.5mm) 16-, 24- and 32-inch circular and double-point needles or size needed to obtain gauge
- Cable needle
- Stitch markers
- Locking stitch markers
- Stitch holders

Gauge

18 sts and 24 rnds = 4 inches/10cm in St st, blocked.

24 sts and 22 rnds = 4 inches/10cm in Mini Cable.

To save time, take time to check gauge.

Special Abbreviations

1 over 1 Left Cross (1/1 LC): Slip 1 to cn and hold in front of work, k1, k1 from cn.

Make 1 (M1): Insert LH needle from front to back under the horizontal thread between the last st worked and next st on LH needle; k1-tbl.

Pattern Stitches

Mini Cable (multiple of 4 sts)
Rnds 1-5: [K2, p2] around.
Rnd 6: [1/1 LC, p2] around.
Rep Rnds 1–6 for pat.

Note: Chart is included for those preferring to work pattern st from a chart.

2x2 Boxes (multiple of 4 sts)
See chart.

3x3 Boxes (multiple of 6 sts)
See chart.

Pattern Notes

The dress is worked in 1 piece from the neck down with raglan increasing for armholes and darts to shape the skirt.

Change to longer circular needle when there are enough stitches to comfortably do so.

Yarn overs are used to increase for the armholes and skirt darts. On every round after increasing, knit each yarn over through the back loop to close hole created by the yarn over.

Measure from neck edge at the center of the front or back to check armhole depth and not along the line of raglan increases.

When increasing, use Make 1 (M1) unless otherwise stated.

Instructions

Shaping Neck

With 16-inch circular needle and MC, cast on 76 (76, 82, 88, 94) sts. Place marker for beg of rnd and join, being careful not to twist sts.

Rnd 1: Knit around.

Rnd 2: K24 (24, 26, 28, 30) for back, yo, k1, yo, k12 (12, 13, 14, 15) for left sleeve, yo, k1, yo, k24 (24, 26, 28, 30) for front, yo, k1, yo, k12 (12, 13, 14, 15) for right sleeve, yo, k1, yo—84 (84, 90, 96, 102) sts.

Place a locking marker on each k1 between yo's to mark position for raglan inc.

Rnd 3: *Knit to yo, k1-tbl, k1, k1-tbl; rep from * 3 more times, knit to end.

Rnd 4: *Knit to marked st, yo, k1, yo; rep from * 3 more times, knit to end—92 (92, 98, 104, 110) sts.

Rep [Rnds 3 and 4] 19 (21, 21, 17, 19) more times—244 (260, 266, 240, 262) sts.

Continue raglan inc on body [every other rnd] 0 (0, 2, 8, 8) more times, and on sleeves every 4 rnds 0 (0, 1, 4, 4) time(s)—244 (260, 278, 288, 310) sts.

Rep [Rnd 3] once more.

Divide for Body & Sleeves

Next rnd: K67 (71, 77, 83, 89) back sts, place next 54 (58, 61, 60, 65) sts on holders or waste yarn for right sleeve; cast on 4 (8, 12, 16, 18) sts for underarm; k68 (72, 78, 84, 90) front sts; place next 54 (58, 61, 60, 65) sts on holders or waste yarn for left sleeve; cast on 4 (8, 12, 16, 18) sts for underarm; place marker for beg of rnd, knit last st—144 (160, 180, 200, 216) sts.

Continue even in St st until body measures 5¼ (5½, 5¾, 6, 6¼) inches from underarm cast-on.

Waist

Change to A. Work [Rnds 1–6] of Mini Cable pat 5 times, then [Rnds 1–5] once more and inc 2 (4, 2, 0, 2) sts evenly around last rnd, making sure to inc in purl sts between cables—146 (164, 182, 200, 218) sts.

Place 4 locking markers for darts as follows: in center of 6th (6th, 7th, 7th, 8th) cable from beg of rnd, in center of 7th (8th, 9th, 11th, 12th) cable from first marker, in center of 11th (12th, 13th, 14th, 15th) cable

from 2nd marker, then in center of 7th (8th, 10th, 11th, 12th) cable from 3rd marker.

Skirt

Change to MC.

Inc rnd 1: *Knit to dart marker, M1; rep from * 3 more times, knit to end—150 (168, 186, 204, 222) sts.

Next rnd: Knit around. Move markers to 4 inc sts from previous rnd.

Inc rnd 2: *Knit to marked st, yo, k1, yo; rep from * 3 more times, knit to end—158 (176, 194, 212, 230) sts.

Next rnd: Knit around. Move markers to 8 new inc sts from previous rnd, adding 4 new markers.

Inc rnd 3: *Knit to marked st, M1, k1, M1; rep from * 7 more times, knit to end—174 (192, 210, 228, 246) sts.

Rep [last 2 rnds] 9 more times—318 (336, 354, 372, 390) sts.

Work even in St st until skirt measures 6 inches.

Change to B. Work even in St st for 3 inches.

Join C. Work in 3x3 Boxes for 4 rnds. Cut B.

With C, work in St st for 4 rnds.

Change to MC. Work in St st for 2 rnds.

Change to B. Work in St st for 4 rnds.

Change to C. Work in St st for 6 rnds, inc 2 (0, 2, 0, 2) sts evenly on last rnd—320 (336, 356, 372, 392) sts.

Change to MC and B. Work in 2x2 Boxes for 4 rnds.

Change to A. Work in St st for 2 rnds.

Change to MC. Work in St st for 4 rnds.

Bind off all sts loosely.

Sleeve

With dpn, cast on 2 (4, 6, 8, 9) sts for underarm, knit sleeve sts from holder, cast on 2 (4, 6, 8, 9) sts for underarm; place marker for beg of rnd and join—58 (66, 73, 76, 83) sts.

Rnd 1: Knit around.

Dec rnd: Ssk, knit to last 2 sts, k2tog—56 (64, 71, 74, 81) sts.

Rep Dec rnd [every other rnd] 0 (2, 5, 3, 6) more times, [every 3 rnds] 2 (2, 0, 2, 0) times—52 (56, 61, 64, 69) sts.

Knit 0 (0, 1, 0, 1) rnd(s) and dec 1 st—52 (56, 60, 64, 68) sts.

Join B. Work in 2x2 Boxes for 2 rnds. Cut B.

With MC, work in St st for 2 rnds. Bind off all sts.

Finishing

Block to measurements. Sew underarm seams. •

MINI CABLE CHART

2X2 BOXES CHART

3X3 BOXES CHART

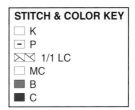

STITCH & COLOR KEY	
☐	K
-	P
⧄	1/1 LC
☐	MC
▨	B
■	C

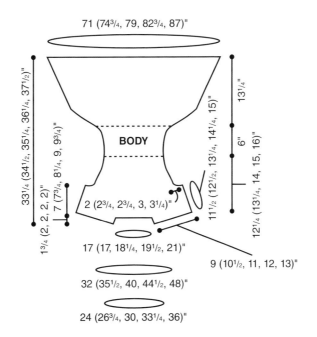

71 (74³/₄, 79, 82³/₄, 87)"

33¹/₄ (34¹/₂, 35¹/₂, 36¹/₄, 37¹/₂)"

7 (7³/₄, 8¹/₄, 9, 9³/₄)"

BODY

13¹/₄"

6"

11¹/₂ (12¹/₂, 13¹/₄, 14¹/₄, 15)"

12¹/₄ (13¹/₄, 14, 15, 16)"

1³/₄ (2, 2, 2, 2)"

2 (2³/₄, 2³/₄, 3, 3¹/₄)"

17 (17, 18¹/₄, 19¹/₂, 21)"

9 (10¹/₂, 11, 12, 13)"

32 (35¹/₂, 40, 44¹/₂, 48)"

24 (26³/₄, 30, 33¹/₄, 36)"

Calliope Cables

Worked from the top down in a lightly textured stockinette stitch, this pullover with a cabled shoulder-hugging yoke, fully fashioned raglans and easy lace is all you need to have a versatile knitting experience.

Design by Joëlle Meier Rioux

Skill Level

■■■■ EXPERIENCED

Sizes

Woman's small (medium, large, extra-large) Instructions are given for the smallest size with larger sizes in parentheses. When only 1 number is given, it applies to all sizes.

Finished Measurements

Chest: 33½ (38, 42, 45¾) inches
Length: 20¼ (20½, 21½, 22¼) inches

Materials

- Rowan Handknit Cotton (DK weight; 100% cotton; 93 yds/50g per skein): 7 (7, 8, 9) skeins ecru #251
- Size 7 (4.5mm) 29-inch circular and double-point needles or size needed to obtain gauge
- Cable needle
- Stitch markers, 1 in CC for beg-of-rnd marker
- Stitch holders

Gauge

21 sts and 30 rnds = 4 inches/10cm in Twisted St st, blocked.

22 sts and 29 rnds = 4 inches/10 cm in Trellis Shell, blocked.

To save time, take time to check gauge.

Special Abbreviations

4 over 4 right cross (4/4 RC): Slip 4 sts to cn and hold in back, k4, k4 from cn.

3 over 3 right cross (3/3 RC): Slip 3 sts to cn and hold in back, k3, k3 from cn.

Pattern Stitches

Twisted St st (multiple of 2 sts)
Rnd 1: *K1, k1-tbl; rep from * around, ending k1 if there is an odd number of sts.
Rnd 2: *K1-tbl, k1; rep from * around, ending k1-tbl if there is an odd number of sts.
Rep Rnds 1 and 2 for Twisted St st.

6-St Yoke Cable (6-st panel)
Row 1 (RS): K6.
Row 2 and all other WS rows: P6.
Row 3: 3/3 RC.
Rows 5 and 7: K6.
Row 8: P6.
Rep Rows 1-8 for 6-St Cable.

8-St Yoke Cable (8-st panel)
Row 1 (RS): K8.
Row 2 and all other WS rows: P8.
Row 3: 4/4 RC.
Rows 5, 7 and 9: K8.
Row 10: P8.
Rep Rows 1–10 for 8-St Cable.

Cabled Yoke Short Row Sequence (31-st panel)
Note: The cables will not cross on the same row every time because of the 2 different cable sizes and the short rows worked to shape the yoke; make sure to keep track of how many rows you have worked on each cable panel since the last cable crossing for that cable.
Row 1 (RS): Work in pat across.
Row 2 (short row; WS): Work 13 sts in pat, W/T.
Row 3 (short row; RS): Work in pat across.
Row 4: Work across, and Pick Up Wrap.
Rows 5–7: Work in pat across.
Row 8 (short row; WS): Work 23 sts in pat, W/T.
Row 9 (short row; RS): Work in pat across.
Row 10: Work across, and Pick Up Wrap.
Rows 11–16: Work in pat across.
Rep Rows 1–16 for Short-Row Sequence.

Trellis Shell (multiple of 13 sts)

Note: The first st of every odd-numbered rnd is used to complete the sk2p at end of rnd; make sure to remove beg of rnd marker before k2tog and replace marker after completed st.

Rnd 1: K1, *k5, yo, k2tog, yo, k1, yo, k2, sk2p; rep from * to last 2 sts, sk2p.

Rnd 2 and all even-numbered rnds: Knit around.

Rnd 3: K1, *k4, yo, k2tog, yo, k3, yo, k1, sk2p; rep from * to last 2 sts, sk2p.

Rnd 5: K1, *k3, yo, k2tog, yo, k5, yo, sk2p; rep from * to last 2 sts, sk2p.

Rnd 7: K1, *k2, yo, k1, yo, ssk, yo, k5, sk2p; rep from * to last 2 sts, sk2p.

Rnd 9: K1, *k1, yo, k3, yo, ssk, yo, k4, sk2p; rep from * to last 2 sts, sk2p.

Rnd 11: K1, *yo, k5, yo, ssk, yo, k3, sk2p; rep from * to last 2 sts, sk2p.

Rnd 12: Knit across.

Rep Rnds 1–12 for Trellis Shell.

Special Techniques

Wrap and Turn (W/T): Work to st indicated. Bring yarn between needles to front of work (or back if already on front). Slip next st pwise. Return yarn to original position. Slip wrapped st back to LH needle without knitting or purling it.

Pick Up Wrap: Work to wrapped st. With tip of needle, lift wrap onto LH needle (from the RS for knit sts and from WS for purl sts). Knit (or purl) next st tog with wrap.

3-Needle Bind-Off: Hold front and back with RS tog and tips of 2 needles facing in same direction. Using a 3rd needle, *insert RH needle into first st on front needle and then first st on back needle and knit these 2 sts tog; rep from * once more and pass first st on RH needle over 2nd st on RH needle. Continue in same manner until all sts are worked tog. Pull yarn through last st.

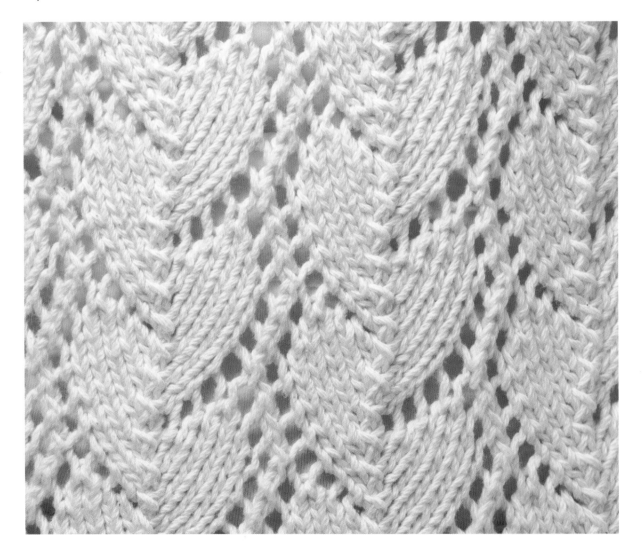

Pattern Notes

This sweater begins with the upper yoke section, which is worked back and forth and shaped with short rows. Stitches for the lower yoke are picked up along lower edge of upper yoke; lower yoke is worked in the round and has raglan shaping to underarm, after which sleeves and body are worked separately down to the bottom edges.

Raglan rounds begin and end at back of the right sleeve.

On the next round, after each raglan increase, knit each yarn over through back of loop; and then on following rounds, work in Twisted Stockinette Stitch pattern.

Instructions

Upper Yoke

Cast on 31 sts.

Set-up row (WS): K2, p8, k4, p8, k2, p6, k1.

Row 1 (RS): Sl 1 wyib, k6, p2, k8, p4, k8, p2.

Row 2: Sl 1 wyif, p8, k4, p8, k2, p6, k1.

Continuing from Row 3 of both cables, beg Short-Row Sequence and work until lower edge of yoke measures approx 38½ (41½, 45, 49) inches from cast-on edge, ending with a WS row so that at least 2 of the 3 cable panels reps look complete when yoke is joined.

With spare needle, pick up 31 loops along cast-on edge. Join ends using 3-Needle Bind-Off; do not cut yarn.

Lower Yoke

With circular needle, beg at rem st, pick up and knit 201 (217, 235, 257) sts evenly around lower edge of yoke—202 (218, 236, 258) sts.

Join to work in rnds.

Set-up rnd: K1, place marker for beg of rnd; *work 33 (33, 36, 41) sts in Twisted St st pat (right sleeve); place raglan marker, k2, place raglan marker; work 64 (72, 78, 84) sts in Twisted St st pat (front); place raglan marker, k2, place raglan marker; rep from * for left sleeve and back, ending at beg of rnd marker.

Rnd 2: Slipping markers as you come to them, *work in Twisted St st pat to next marker, p2; rep from * 3 more times.

Rnd 3 (inc): *Yo, work in established pat to next marker, yo, slip marker, k2, slip marker; rep from * 3 more times—210 (226, 244, 266) sts.

Continuing in established pat, inc [every 5 rnds] 0 (6, 7, 8) more times, then [every 4 rnds] 5 (0, 0, 0) times—250 (274, 300, 330) sts.

Work even until lower yoke measures 4¾ (5, 5½, 6¼) inches from pick-up rnd.

Divide for Body & Sleeves
Removing markers as you work, place last st and first 46 (48, 53, 60) sts on holders or waste yarn for right sleeve, cast on 5 (6, 7, 8) sts for underarm, work in established pat across next 78 (88, 96, 104) sts for front, place next 47 (49, 54, 61) sts on holders or waste yarn for left sleeve, cast on 10 (12, 14, 16) sts for underarm, work across next 78 (88, 96, 104) sts for back, then cast on 5 (6, 7, 8) sts—176 (200, 220, 240) sts.

Working new sts in established pat, continue even for 1½ (1½, 2, 2) inches.

Set up lace
Inc rnd: Knit around, inc 6 (8, 1, 7) st(s) evenly around—182 (208, 221, 247) sts.

Work in Trellis Shell pat until body measures approx 11½ (11½, 12, 12) inches from underarm cast-on, ending with an even-numbered rnd.

Next rnd: Purl around.

Next rnd: Knit around.

Bind off pwise.

Sleeves
With dpn, cast on 5 (6, 7, 8) sts, work in established pat over 47 (49, 54, 61) sleeve sts, cast on 5 (6, 7, 8) sts—57 (61, 68, 77) sts.

Place marker for beg of rnd and join.

Working new sts in pat, continue in established pat until sleeve measures 1½ (1½, 2, 2) inches from underarm cast-on.

Next rnd: Purl around.

Bind off all sts kwise.

Finishing
Block to finished measurements. Sew underarm seams. ●

STITCH KEY

☐ K on RS, p on WS
⊟ P on RS, k on Ws
☑ sl 1 wyib on RS, sl 1 wyif on WS
⤬ 3/3 RC
⤬ 4/4 RC
Ⓞ Yo
◺ K2tog
◹ Ssk
⋉ sl 1, k2tog, psso

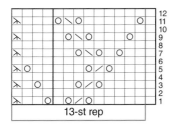

13-st rep

TRELLIS SHELL CHART

Note: Sk2p at end of last rep uses first st of rnd; be sure to remove beg of rnd marker before working the last sk2p, and replace marker for new beg of rnd.

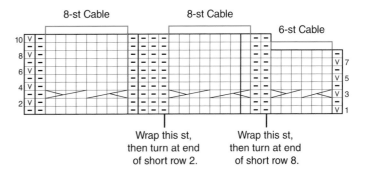

8-st Cable   8-st Cable   6-st Cable

Wrap this st, then turn at end of short row 2.

Wrap this st, then turn at end of short row 8.

CABLE PANELS & SHORT-ROW SEQUENCE CHART

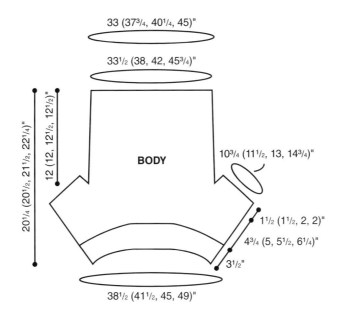

33 (37¾, 40¼, 45)"

33½ (38, 42, 45¾)"

20¼ (20½, 21½, 22¼)"

12 (12, 12½, 12½)"

BODY

10¾ (11½, 13, 14¾)"

1½ (1½, 2, 2)"

4¾ (5, 5½, 6¼)"

3½"

38½ (41½, 45, 49)"

off the **cuff**

Stretch your imagination and view your projects from a new perspective.

We've addressed many of the fundamentals of knitting on circular needles, and now it's time to mix things up and take things in a whole new direction.

In the example below, we begin our cast-on edge at the left cuff and work back and forth. When the sleeve is complete, stitches are cast on for the front and back, which are worked simultaneously to the back neck, after which they are worked separately to create the front opening. After the neck is complete, right front stitches are cast on, and the back and front are worked simultaneously again. Finally, the right sleeve is worked down to the cuff. In many respects we can compare the benefits of this method of knitting to working in the round because the entire garment is worked in one piece, making the process fluid and less static than other forms of back and forth knitting. Additionally, a back and forth, cuff to cuff garment is more dynamic than its traditional "in pieces" counterpart, because you can "try on as you go," instead of making four separate body units and hoping for the best. Another benefit to working cuff to cuff is that the stitch and color patterns are vertical on the body instead of horizontal, creating a nice slimming effect.

In the next example, both in-the-round and flat knitting methods are utilized. In the diagram below, the directional arrows indicate that each sleeve and half-yoke is worked separately from the cuff to the center back. After the two pieces are joined at the center, the body is worked in the round from the yoke downward.

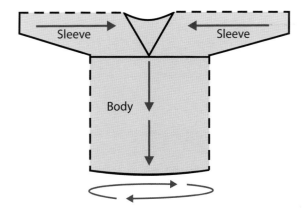

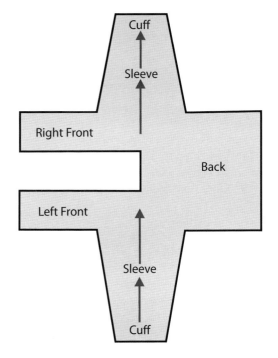

T!P

HOW TO If you need to transfer stitches to a stitch holder or waste yarn, try using a spare circular needle the same size or smaller than your main needle. If you're concerned about stitches falling off the end of the needle, place a needle guard at each end. When you're ready to work the stitches, knit directly off the spare needle. This saves the time of transferring your stitches from a stitch holder or waste yarn back to a needle. If you need to place stitches for your sleeves onto holders before working a yoke, use shorter spare circular needles for each sleeve.

Just the Right Jacket

The fashion-forward design, along with impressive shaping details, makes this piece a must for your wardrobe.

Design by Pauline Schultz

∙∙

Skill Level

◼◼◼◻ INTERMEDIATE

Sizes

Woman's small (medium, large, extra-large, 2X-large, 3X-large, 4X-large) Instructions are given for smallest size, with larger sizes in parentheses. When only 1 number is given, it applies to all sizes.

Finished Measurements

Chest: 36 (39, 44, 48, 52, 56, 60) inches
Length: 20½ (20¾, 20¾, 21, 21, 21¼, 21¼) inches

Materials

- Shibui Knits Merino Kid (DK weight; 55% kid mohair/45% merino wool; 218 yds/100g per skein): 6 (7, 8, 8, 9, 10, 11) skeins honey #1395

3 LIGHT

- Size 3 (3.25mm) 24- or 36-inch circular needle or size needed to obtain gauge
- 2 size 6 (4mm) 24- or 36-inch circular needles or size needed to obtain gauge
- Size G/6 (4mm) crochet hook
- Stitch markers

Gauge

26 sts and 34 rows = 4 inches/10cm in k1, p1 rib with smaller needle.

21 sts and 38 rows = 4 inches/10cm in Basket Weave pat with larger needle, blocked.

To save time, take time to check gauge.

Pattern Stitch

Basket Weave (multiple of 6 sts + 8)
Row 1 and all WS rows: Knit.
Rows 2 (RS) and 4: P2, *k4, p2; rep from * to end.

Rows 6 and 8: K3, *p2, k4; rep from * to last 5 sts, p2, k3.
Rep Rows 1–8 for pat.

Special Techniques

Crochet Cast-On: Make slip knot on crochet hook. *Hold crochet hook vertically in front of and at right angles to the needle with the needle point facing right. Take the yarn under the needle, up and across the front of the crochet hook. Pull yarn through loop—new st on needle. Rep from * as required. Slip loop from crochet hook to needle to form the last st.

Provisional Cast-On: With crochet hook and waste yarn, make a chain several sts longer than desired cast-on. With knitting needle and project yarn, pick up indicated number of sts in the "bumps" on back of chain. When indicated in pat, "unzip" the crochet chain to free live sts.

3-Needle Bind-Off: Hold front and back with RS tog and tips of 2 needles facing in same direction. Using a 3rd needle, *insert RH needle into first st on front needle and then first st on back needle and knit these 2 sts tog; rep from * once more and pass first st on RH needle over 2nd st on RH needle. Continue in same manner until all sts are worked tog. Pull yarn through last st.

Pattern Notes

This jacket is worked in 1 piece from cuff to cuff. The lower edge of the body is worked in garter stitch and side seams are joined using 3-Needle Bind-Off. The shawl collar is worked after the main sweater is complete.

To maximize the subtle color changes of hand-painted yarn and avoid slight differences between skeins, work with 2 skeins at once, alternating strands every 2 rows. When working the ribbed sleeves, change strands at the edge; when working the body, change strands at the top shoulder

because this will help to reinforce the shoulder and back neck. When working the collar, change strands at the center back on the right side (RS) of garment (collar will fold back, hiding the strand change).

When establishing the Basket Weave pattern on the body, the first row will not end with a complete repeat for sizes small (extra-large, 2X-large, 3X-large, 4X-large). For these sizes, work the last 7 (1, 1, 1, 1) stitch(es) into the pattern as given; the pattern repeat will work correctly on the next wrong-side row after the back stitches have been cast on.

Instructions

First Sleeve

With smaller needle, using Crochet Cast-On method, cast on 110 (112, 112, 114, 114, 114, 114) sts.

Work in k1, p1 rib until sleeve measures 8 (8½, 8¾, 9, 9¼, 9½, 9¾) inches or desired length, ending with a RS row.

Body

Row 1 (WS): Change to larger needle; bind off 1 st, work in rib to end of row—109 (111, 111, 113, 113, 113, 113) sts.

Row 2: Bind off 1 st, knit to end of row, then using Provisional Cast-On method, cast on 54 (54, 54, 54, 54, 55, 55) front sts—162 (164, 164, 166, 166, 167, 167) sts.

Row 3: K5 (6, 6, 7, 7, 8, 8), place marker, beg with Row 2 of Basket Weave pat, work across row, then provisionally cast on 54 (54, 54, 54, 54, 55, 55) back sts—216 (218, 218, 220, 220, 222, 222) sts.

Row 4: K5 (6, 6, 7, 7, 8, 8), place marker, work in pat to marker, knit to end of row.

Maintaining first and last 5 (6, 6, 7, 7, 8, 8) sts in garter st, work even until body measures 6½ (7, 8¼, 9¼, 10¼, 11, 12) inches, ending with a WS row.

Divide for back neck

Next row (RS): Work 108 (109, 109, 110, 110, 111, 111) back sts, turn and slip rem 108 (109, 109, 110, 110, 111, 111) front sts to waste yarn.

Work even on back sts for 5 (5½, 5½, 5½, 5½, 6, 6) inches, ending with a WS row.

Next row (RS): Work back sts to neck edge, then provisionally cast on 108 (109, 109, 110, 110, 111, 111) front sts, placing marker before last 5 (6, 6, 7, 7, 8, 8) sts—216 (218, 218, 220, 220, 222, 222) sts.

Maintaining first and last 5 (6, 6, 7, 7, 8, 8) sts in garter st, work even until front measures 6½ (7, 8¼, 9¼, 10¼, 11, 12) inches, ending with a WS row.

Next row (RS): Work 162 (164, 164, 166, 166, 167, 167) sts, slip rem front 54 (54, 54, 54, 54, 55, 55) front sts to waste yarn; turn.

Next row: Work 108 (110, 110, 112, 112, 112, 112) sleeve sts, slip rem 54 (54, 54, 54, 54, 55, 55) back sts to waste yarn; turn.

Second Sleeve
Next row (RS): Change to smaller needle. Work in k1, p1 rib and inc 1 st at beg and end of row—110 (112, 112, 114, 114, 114, 114) sts.

Continue in rib until sleeve measures 8 (8½, 8¾, 9, 9¼, 9½, 9¾) inches, or same length as first sleeve.

Bind off loosely in rib.

Finishing
Weave in ends. Block to finished measurements.

Transfer right front and back side sts to larger needle, with each set of sts at opposite ends of needle. Join using 3-Needle Bind-Off.

Rep for left side seam.

Sew sleeve seams.

Collar
Unzip right front cast-on and place live sts on larger needle; place left front sts from waste yarn on larger needle.

With RS facing, work p1, k1 rib across right front sts, pick up and knit 27 (27, 29, 29, 31, 31, 33) sts across back neck, continue in rib across left front sts to end of row—243 (245, 247, 249, 251, 253, 255) sts.

Continue in rib for 4 (4½, 5, 6, 7, 7½, 8) inches.

Bind off very loosely in rib.

Weave in rem ends. ●

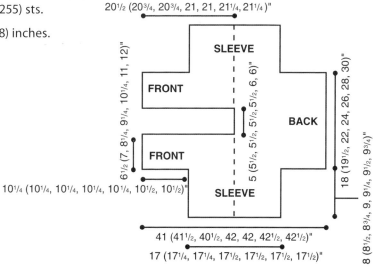

20½ (20¾, 20¾, 21, 21, 21¼, 21¼)"

SLEEVE

FRONT

6½ (7, 8¼, 9¼, 10¼, 11, 12)"

FRONT

5 (5½, 5½, 5½, 6, 6)"

BACK

SLEEVE

18 (19½, 22, 24, 26, 28, 30)"

10¼ (10¼, 10¼, 10¼, 10¼, 10½, 10½)"

41 (41½, 40½, 42, 42, 42½, 42½)"

17 (17¼, 17¼, 17½, 17½, 17½, 17½)"

8 (8½, 8¾, 9, 9¼, 9½, 9¾)"

Lavinia Long-Sleeved Tee

Just because a garment is knit in the round and is seamless doesn't mean there can't be some "faux seams" that give the garment style and design lines. This sweater is partly knit from side to side and partly knit up and down. The yarn makes subtle stripes that are emphasized by the multidirectional knitting.

Design by Lorna Miser

Skill Level
■■■□ INTERMEDIATE

Sizes
Woman's small (medium, large, extra-large) Instructions are given for smallest size, with larger sizes in parentheses. When only 1 number is given, it applies to all sizes.

Finished Measurements
Chest: 33½ (37¼, 41, 44¾) inches
Length: 22 (23, 24, 25) inches

Materials
- Manos del Uruguay Wool Clasica Naturals (heavy worsted weight; 100% wool; 138 yds/100g per skein): 5 (5, 6, 6) skeins lime #706
- Size 9 (5.5mm) 16- and 32-inch circular and double-point needles or size needed to obtain gauge
- Stitch markers
- Stitch holder

Gauge
15 sts and 19 rows = 4 inches/10cm in St st, blocked.

To save time, take time to check gauge.

Special Abbreviation
Make 1 (M1): Insert LH needle from front to back under the horizontal thread between the last st worked and next st on LH needle; k1-tbl.

Pattern Stitch
Garter St (worked in the rnd)
Rnd 1: Purl around.
Rnd 2: Knit around.
Rep [Rnds 1 and 2] for pat.

Pattern Notes
The top portion of this sweater is worked from cuff to cuff; work begins in the round at the left sleeve cuff, splits for the front and back yoke, then rejoins to work in the round to the right sleeve cuff.

Change to circular needles when number of stitches allows.

The body stitches are picked up along the edges of the yoke and knit down.

Instructions

Left Sleeve
With dpn, cast on 28 (30, 32, 34) sts. Place marker for beg of rnd and join, taking care not to twist sts.

Work 5 rnds garter st, ending with a purl rnd.

Inc rnd: Knit and inc 4 (4, 6, 8) sts evenly around—32 (34, 38, 42) sts.

Work even in St st for 4 rnds.

Inc rnd: K1, M1, knit to last st, M1, k1—34 (36, 40, 44 sts).

Rep Inc rnd [every 5 rnds] 15 more times—64 (66, 70, 74) sts.

Work even until sleeve measures 18¾ (18¾, 19¼, 19¼) inches from cast-on edge, making note of number of rnds worked after last inc. Place marker for underarm.

Divide for Yoke & Left Shoulder

Beg working back and forth. Work even in St st until yoke measures 4¼ (5¼, 6¼, 7¼) inches from marker, ending with a WS row.

Shape front neck

Row 1 (RS): K32 (33, 35, 37) sts and place on holder for back, bind off 6 sts for side neck, knit to end—26 (27, 29, 31) sts.

Row 2: Purl across.

Dec row (RS): K1, ssk, knit to end—25 (26, 28, 30) sts.

Rep [last 2 rows] 3 more times—22 (23, 25, 27) sts.

Work even for 4½ inches, ending with a WS row.

Inc row (RS): K1, M1, knit to end—23 (24, 26, 28) sts.

Next row: Purl across.

Rep [last 2 rows] 3 more times—26 (27, 29, 31) sts.

Next row (WS): Purl across, then using Cable Cast-On method (see page 58), cast on 6 sts—32 (33, 35, 37) sts.

Place front sts on holder or waste yarn.

Shape back neck

With RS facing and continuing in St st, join yarn for back yoke—32 (33, 35, 37) sts.

Work even in St st for 8 inches, ending with a WS row.

Right Shoulder

Next row (RS): Work across back sts, then knit front sts from holder—64 (66, 70, 74) sts.

Continue even in St st for 4¼ (5¼, 6¼, 7¼) inches. Place marker for underarm.

Right Sleeve

Place marker for beg of rnd and join.

Work even for the same number of rnds as were worked after last inc for left sleeve.

Dec rnd: K1, ssk, knit to last 3 sts, k2tog, k1—62 (64, 68, 72) sts.

Continuing in St st, rep Dec rnd [every 5 rnds] 15 more times—32 (34, 38, 42) sts.

Work even until sleeve measures approx 17¾ (17¾, 18¼, 18¼) inches from marker.

Dec rnd: Knit and dec 4 (4, 6, 8) sts evenly around—28 (30, 32, 34) sts.

Work 5 rnds garter st, ending with a purl rnd.

Bind off all sts kwise.

Neckband

With 16-inch circular needle, pick up and knit 64 sts around neck edge. Place marker for beg of rnd and join.

Work 4 rnds garter st.

Bind off all sts pwise.

Body

With longer circular needle, beg at one underarm marker, pick up and knit 126 (140, 154, 168) sts around yoke. Place marker for beg of rnd and join.

Work in St st until body measures approx 12½ (13¼, 13¾, 14¼) inches from underarm.

Work 4 rnds garter st.

Bind off all sts loosely pwise.

Finishing

Block to measurements. ●

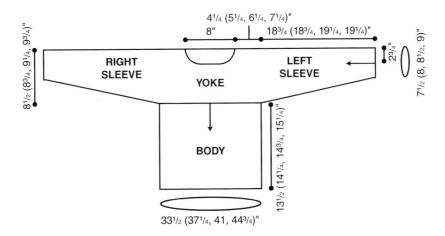

Aurora

Add some glam to your wardrobe with this boldly striped shrug. The addition of the short-row collar adds dimension and intrigue.

Design by Ann Weaver

Skill Level
■■■□ INTERMEDIATE

Sizes
Woman's extra-small (small/medium, medium/large, large/extra-large) Instructions are given for smallest size, with larger sizes in parentheses. When only 1 number is given, it applies to all sizes.

Finished Measurements
Back width (between sleeves): 14¾ (16, 17, 17¾) inches
Sleeve length: 15 (16, 16½, 17¼) inches

Materials
- Manos del Uruguay Silk Blend Semi Solids (DK weight; 70% merino/30% silk; 150 yds/50g per skein): 3 (4, 4, 4) skeins black #3008 (MC) and 2 (3, 3, 3) skeins rust #300U (CC)
- Size 4 (3.5mm) double-point needles (set of 4) or size needed to obtain gauge
- Size 6 (4mm) 16- and 24-inch circular and double-point needles (set of 5) or size needed to obtain gauge
- Stitch markers, 1 in CC for beg of rnd
- Locking stitch markers

Gauge
23 sts and 34 rnds = 4 inches/10cm in St st using larger needles.

To save time, take time to check gauge.

Special Abbreviations
Make 1 (M1): Insert LH needle from front to back under horizontal thread between last st worked and next st on LH needle; k1-tbl.

N1, N2, N3, N4: Needle 1, Needle 2, Needle 3, Needle 4.

Pattern Stitches
K1, P1 Rib (even number of sts)
Pat rnd: *K1, p1; rep from * around.
Rep Pat rnd for pat.

Stripe Sequence
*Work 25 (27, 29, 30) rnds/rows CC in St st.
Work 25 (27, 29, 30) rnds/rows MC in St st.
Rep from * for pat.

Special Techniques
Wrap and Turn (W/T): Work to st indicated. Bring yarn between needles to front of work (or back if already on front). Slip next st pwise. Return yarn to original position. Slip wrapped st back to left needle without knitting or purling it.

Pick Up Wrap: Work to wrapped st. With tip of needle, lift wrap onto LH needle (from the RS for knit sts and from WS for purl sts). Knit (or purl) next st tog with the wrap.

Pattern Notes
This shrug is worked from side to side, beginning in the round at the left sleeve cuff, dividing and working flat for the back, and then rejoining and working the right sleeve in the round.

Change to circular needle when the number of stitches allows, and back to double-point needles when there are too few stitches to work on the circular needle.

Instructions

Left Sleeve
With smaller dpn and MC, cast on 52 (58, 64, 70) sts. Distribute sts with 13 (14, 16, 17) sts on N1; 13 (15, 16, 18) sts on N2; 13 (14, 16, 17) sts on N3; and 13 (15, 16, 18) sts on N4. Place marker for beg of rnd and join, taking care not to twist sts.

Work in K1, P1 Rib until piece measures 6¼ (6½, 6¼, 6¾) inches.

Change to CC, larger dpn and St st.

Work 25 (27, 29, 30) rnds in Stripe pat.

Inc rnd: Continuing Stripe pat, k2, M1, knit to last st, M1, k1—54 (60, 66, 72) sts.

Work even for 7 (7, 9, 9) rnds.

Rep [last 8 (8, 10, 10) rnds] once more, then rep Inc rnd—58 (64, 70, 76) sts.

Work even for 8 (10, 8, 9) rnds.

Underarm gusset
Continue in Stripe pat.

Set-up rnd: K1, M1, place marker for underarm gusset, knit to end of rnd, place marker for underarm gusset, M1—60 (66, 72, 78) sts with 3 sts between gusset markers.

Work even for 2 rnds.

Inc rnd: Knit to gusset marker, M1, slip marker, knit to gusset marker, slip marker, M1, knit to end of rnd—62 (68, 74, 80) sts with 5 sts between gusset markers.

Rep [last 3 rnds] 6 (7, 7, 8) more times—74 (82, 88, 96) sts with 17 (19, 19, 21) sts between gusset markers.

Work even for 2 (1, 3, 1) rnd(s).

Next rnd: Knit to 2nd gusset marker, bind off 17 (19, 19, 21) gusset sts—57 (63, 69, 75) sts.

Back
Continuing in Stripe pat and working back and forth, work even for 125 (135, 145, 150) rows (5 stripes are completed on back); back should measure approx 14¾ (16, 17, 17¾) inches from gusset bind-off.

Right Sleeve
Next row (RS): Continuing in Stripe pat, knit to end, then, place marker for underarm gusset, cast on 17 (19, 19, 21) sts for underarm gusset, place marker for gusset—74 (82, 88, 96) sts.

Work even for 2 (1, 3, 1) rnd(s).

Dec rnd: Knit to gusset marker, ssk, knit to 2 sts before gusset marker, k2tog—72 (80, 86, 94) sts with 15 (17, 17, 19) sts between gusset markers.

Work even for 2 rnds.

Rep [last 3 rnds] 6 (7, 7, 8) more times, then rep Dec rnd—58 (64, 70, 76) sts with 1 st between gusset markers.

Continuing in Stripe pat, knit to first gusset marker, remove marker, then knit rem st; rem marker is for beg of rnd.

Work even for 7 (9, 7, 8) rnds.

Dec rnd: K2, k2tog, knit to last 3 sts, ssk, k1— 56 (62, 68, 74) sts.

Work even for 7 (7, 9, 9) rnds.

Rep [last 8 (8, 10, 10) rnds] once more, then rep Dec rnd—52 (58, 64, 70) sts.

Work 25 (27, 29, 30) rnds for last stripe.

Change to smaller dpns and MC.

Work even in K1, P1 Rib for approx 6¼ (6½, 6¼, 6¾) inches.

Bind off all sts loosely in rib.

Place markers in 1 side edge of body opening at end of each gusset for upper (neck) edge of back.

Border
With longer circular needle and MC, beg below marker at left sleeve, pick up and knit 16 (18, 18, 20) sts in left sleeve gusset, 80 (90, 96, 100) sts along lower edge of back, 16 (18, 18, 20) sts along right sleeve gusset, place marker, then pick up and knit 80 (90, 96, 100) sts along upper edge of back—192 (216, 228, 240) sts.

Place marker for beg of rnd, and join.

Work K1, P1 Rib for 3 inches.

Bind off loosely in rib to first marker—80 (90, 96, 100) upper back sts rem.

Collar
Change to CC.

Continuing back and forth in established rib, shape collar using short rows as follows:

Row 1 (RS): Work to last 4 sts, W/T.

Row 2: Work to last 4 sts, W/T.

Row 3: Work to 3 sts before wrapped st, W/T.

Rep [Row 3] 13 more times, ending with a WS row with 30 (40, 46, 50) sts rem in work between wraps.

Next row: Work across to the end of the row, working wraps tog with wrapped sts.

Rep last row.

Bind off all sts loosely in rib.

Finishing
Block to measurements. ●

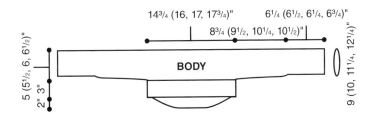

14¾ (16, 17, 17¾)"   6¼ (6½, 6¼, 6¾)"

8¾ (9½, 10¼, 10½)"

9 (10, 11¼, 12¼)"

5 (5½, 6, 6½)"

2"   3"

BODY

General Information

Abbreviations & Symbols

[ ] work instructions within brackets as many times as directed

( ) work instructions within parentheses in the place directed

** repeat instructions following the asterisks as directed

* repeat instructions following the single asterisk as directed

" inch(es)

approx approximately
beg begin/begins/beginning
CC contrasting color
ch chain stitch
cm centimeter(s)
cn cable needle
dec decrease/decreases/decreasing
dpn(s) double-point needle(s)
g gram(s)
inc increase/increases/increasing

k knit
k2tog knit 2 stitches together
kwise knitwise
LH left hand
m meter(s)
M1 make one stitch
MC main color
mm millimeter(s)
oz ounce(s)
p purl
pat(s) pattern(s)
p2tog purl 2 stitches together
psso pass slipped stitch over
pwise purlwise
rem remain/remains/remaining
rep repeat(s)
rev St st reverse stockinette stitch
RH right hand
rnd(s) rounds
RS right side
skp slip, knit, pass slipped stitch over—1 stitch decreased

sk2p slip 1, knit 2 together, pass slipped stitch over the knit 2 together—2 stitches decreased
sl slip
sl 1kwise slip 1 knitwise
sl 1pwise slip 1 purlwise
sl st slip stitch(es)
ssk slip, slip, knit these 2 stitches together—a decrease
st(s) stitch(es)
St st stockinette stitch
tbl through back loop(s)
tog together
WS wrong side
wyib with yarn in back
wyif with yarn in front
yd(s) yard(s)
yfwd yarn forward
yo (yo's) yarn over(s)

Skill Levels

BEGINNER

Beginner projects for first-time knitters using basic stitches. Minimal shaping.

EASY

Easy projects using basic stitches, repetitive stitch patterns, simple color changes and simple shaping and finishing.

INTERMEDIATE

Intermediate projects with a variety of stitches, mid-level shaping and finishing.

EXPERIENCED

Experienced projects using advanced techniques and stitches, detailed shaping and refined finishing.

Standard Yarn Weight System
Categories of yarn, gauge ranges, and recommended needle sizes

Yarn Weight Symbol & Category Names	① SUPER FINE	② FINE	③ LIGHT	④ MEDIUM	⑤ BULKY	⑥ SUPER BULKY
Type of Yarns in Category	Sock, Fingering, Baby	Sport, Baby	DK, Light Worsted	Worsted, Afghan, Aran	Chunky, Craft, Rug	Bulky, Roving
Knit Gauge Range* in Stockinette Stitch to 4 inches	27–32 sts	23–26 sts	21–24 sts	16–20 sts	12–15 sts	6–11 sts
Recommended Needle in Metric Size Range	2.25–3.25mm	3.25–3.75mm	3.75–4.5mm	4.5–5.5mm	5.5–8mm	8mm and larger
Recommended Needle U.S. Size Range	1 to 3	3 to 5	5 to 7	7 to 9	9 to 11	11 and larger

* **GUIDELINES ONLY:** The above reflect the most commonly used gauges and needle sizes for specific yarn categories.

Inches Into Millimeters & Centimeters
All measurements are rounded off slightly.

inches	mm	cm	inches	cm	inches	cm	inches	cm
⅛	3	0.3	5	12.5	21	53.5	38	96.5
¼	6	0.6	5½	14	22	56.0	39	99.0
⅜	10	1.0	6	15.0	23	58.5	40	101.5
½	13	1.3	7	18.0	24	61.0	41	104.0
⅝	15	1.5	8	20.5	25	63.5	42	106.5
¾	20	2.0	9	23.0	26	66.0	43	109.0
⅞	22	2.2	10	25.5	27	68.5	44	112.0
1	25	2.5	11	28.0	28	71.0	45	114.5
1¼	32	3.2	12	30.5	29	73.5	46	117.0
1½	38	3.8	13	33.0	30	76.0	47	119.5
1¾	45	4.5	14	35.5	31	79.0	48	122.0
2	50	5.0	15	38.0	32	81.5	49	124.5
2½	65	6.5	16	40.5	33	84.0	50	127.0
3	75	7.5	17	43.0	34	86.5		
3½	90	9.0	18	46.0	35	89.0		
4	100	10.0	19	48.5	36	91.5		
4½	115	11.5	20	51.0	37	94.0		

Knitting Basics

Cast-On

Leaving an end about an inch long for each stitch to be cast on, make a slip knot on the right needle.

Place the thumb and index finger of your left hand between the yarn ends with the long yarn end over your thumb, and the strand from the skein over your index finger. Close your other fingers over the strands to hold them against your palm. Spread your thumb and index fingers apart and draw the yarn into a "V."

Place the needle in front of the strand around your thumb and bring it underneath this strand. Carry the needle over and under the strand on your index finger.

Draw through loop on thumb.

Drop the loop from your thumb and draw up the strand to form a stitch on the needle.

Repeat until you have cast on the number of stitches indicated in the pattern. Remember to count the beginning slip knot as a stitch.

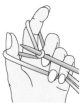

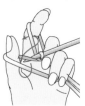

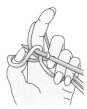

Cable Cast-On

This type of cast-on is used when adding stitches in the middle or at the end of a row.

Make a slip knot on the left needle. Knit a stitch in this knot and place it on the left needle. Insert the right needle between the last two stitches on the left needle. Knit a stitch and place it on the left needle. Repeat for each stitch needed.

Knit (k)

Insert tip of right needle from front to back in next stitch on left needle.

Bring yarn under and over the tip of the right needle.

Pull yarn loop through the stitch with right needle point.

Slide the stitch off the left needle. The new stitch is on the right needle.

Purl (p)

With yarn in front, insert tip of right needle from back to front through next stitch on the left needle.

Bring yarn around the right needle counterclockwise.

With right needle, draw yarn back through the stitch.

Slide the stitch off the left needle. The new stitch is on the right needle.

Bind-Off

Binding off (knit)

Knit first two stitches on left needle. Insert tip of left needle into first stitch worked on right needle and pull it over the second stitch and completely off the needle.

Knit the next stitch and repeat. When one stitch remains on right needle, cut yarn and draw tail through last stitch to fasten off.

Binding off (purl)

Purl first two stitches on left needle. Insert tip of left needle into first stitch worked on right needle and pull it over the second stitch and completely off the needle.

Purl the next stitch and repeat. When one stitch remains on right needle, cut yarn and draw tail through last stitch to fasten off.

Increase (inc)

Two stitches in one stitch

Increase (knit)

Knit the next stitch in the usual manner, but don't remove the stitch from the left needle. Place right needle behind left needle and knit again into the back of the same stitch. Slip original stitch off left needle.

Increase (purl)

Purl the next stitch in the usual manner, but don't remove the stitch from the left needle. Place right needle behind left needle and purl again into the back of the same stitch. Slip original stitch off left needle.

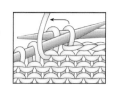

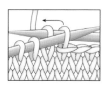

Invisible Increase (M1)
There are several ways to make or increase one stitch.

Make 1 with Left Twist (M1L)
Insert left needle from front to back under the horizontal loop between the last stitch worked and next stitch on left needle.

With right needle, knit into the back of this loop.

To make this increase on the purl side, insert left needle in same manner and purl into the back of the loop.

Make 1 with Right Twist (M1R)
Insert left needle from back to front under the horizontal loop between the last stitch worked and next stitch on left needle.

With right needle, knit into the front of this loop.

To make this increase on the purl side, insert left needle in same manner and purl into the front of the loop.

Make 1 with Backward Loop over the right needle
With your thumb, make a loop over the right needle.

Slip the loop from your thumb onto the needle and pull to tighten.

Make 1 in top of stitch below
Insert tip of right needle into the stitch on left needle one row below.

Knit this stitch, then knit the stitch on the left needle.

Decrease (dec)

Knit 2 together (k2tog)
Put tip of right needle through next two stitches on left needle as to knit. Knit these two stitches as one.

Purl 2 together (p2tog)
Put tip of right needle through next two stitches on left needle as to purl. Purl these two stitches as one.

Slip, Slip, Knit (ssk)
Slip next two stitches, one at a time, as to knit from left needle to right needle.

Insert left needle in front of both stitches and work off needle together.

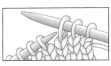

Slip, Slip, Purl (ssp)
Slip next two stitches, one at a time, as to knit from left needle to right needle. Slip these stitches back onto left needle keeping them twisted. Purl these two stitches together through back loops.

Kitchener Stitch
This method of weaving with two needles is used for the toes of socks and flat seams. To weave the edges together and form an unbroken line of stockinette stitch, divide all stitches evenly onto two knitting needles—one behind the other. Thread yarn into tapestry needle. Hold needles with wrong sides together and work from right to left as follows:

Step 1: Insert tapestry needle into first stitch on front needle as to purl. Draw yarn through stitch, leaving stitch on knitting needle.

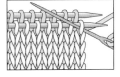

Step 2: Insert tapestry needle into the first stitch on the back needle as to purl. Draw yarn through stitch and slip stitch off knitting needle.

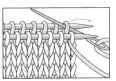

Step 3: Insert tapestry needle into the next stitch on same (back) needle as to knit, leaving stitch on knitting needle.

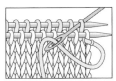

Step 4: Insert tapestry needle into the first stitch on the front needle as to knit. Draw yarn through stitch and slip stitch off knitting needle.

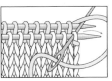

Step 5: Insert tapestry needle into the next stitch on same (front) needle as to purl. Draw yarn through stitch, leaving stitch on knitting needle.

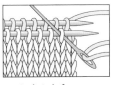

Repeat Steps 2 through 5 until one stitch is left on each needle. Then repeat Steps 2 and 4. Fasten off. Woven stitches should be the same size as adjacent knitted stitches.

Working With Double-Point Needles (dpn)

Double-point needles come in sets of four or five and are usually European made. With these, the work is divided evenly among three or four needles, with the fourth or fifth being 6–9 inches. Very short (4-inch) needles are available from specialty sources and are often known as glove or finger needles. These are especially useful when working thumbs on gloves or mittens.

If you are new to working with double-point needles, it may feel awkward at first. This is normal, and as with any new endeavor, will go away with time as you become more comfortable manipulating multiple needles.

Casting on

Cast on one-third the desired number of stitches onto the first needle. Holding the second needle parallel and below the first, cast on another one-third of the stitches. Hold the third needle parallel below the first two and cast on the remaining one-third. Photo 1 shows 10 stitches cast onto each needle. *Tip: If you prefer, you can also cast on all of your stitches onto a straight needle, then transfer the stitches to each separate double-point needle.*

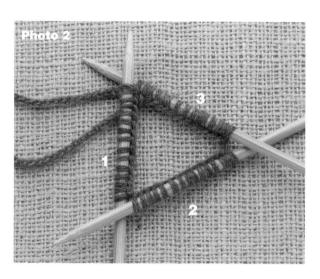

Photo 2

Arranging the Needles

Rearrange the needles to form a triangle, with the base closest to you and the point facing away. All the stitches are at the bottom of the needles and should not be twisted. Both the tail end and the end of yarn connected to the skein are at the left end of needle 3 (see Photo 2). If you're using four needles, rearrange the needles to form a square so that the tail end and the end of yarn connected to the skein are at the left end of needle 4.

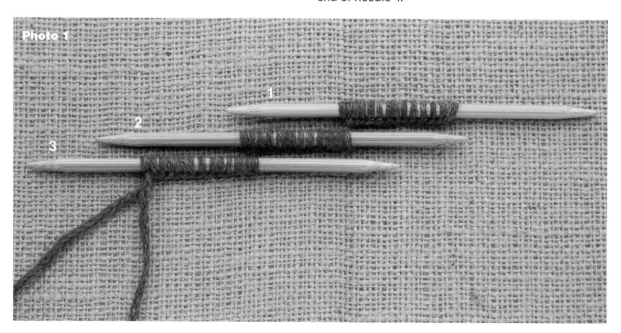

Photo 1

60

Slip the first stitch from needle 1 and place onto needle 3. Slip the ending stitch from needle 3 up and over the stitch just transferred onto needle 1 to "join" into a ring.

Using the end of yarn connected to the skein and the fourth (free) needle, knit the stitches on the first needle. When all stitches are on the new needle, the needle that formerly held the stitches now becomes the free needle. Continue turning the work, so you are always working at the "base" of the triangle. The yarn tail will mark the beginning of needle 1. To avoid a "ladder" of larger stitches from forming when you change from one needle to the next, work the first stitch of each needle a bit tighter than usual.

Photo 3 shows a cuff being worked in K1, P1 ribbing. Our sample of 30 stitches works out rather nicely with 10 stitches per needle. In K1, P1 ribbing, this means there will always be a starting needle with a knit, and ending with a purl, exactly even with the pattern.

Photo 3

But what about a cuff with 32 stitches worked in K2, P2 rib? Dividing by three doesn't work out evenly. We could put 11 stitches on each of the first two needles and 10 on the last, which translates beginning needle 1 with K2 and end with P1. Needle 2 would begin with P1 and end with K2, while needle 3 would begin and end with P2, making it hard to develop a knitting rhythm, but easy to make a mistake. The solution is to rearrange the stitches so we have 12 stitches each on the first and last needles, and eight on the second. With all numbers being multiples of four, you can work around the cuff in K2, P2 ribbing, always coming out even.

Working With Two Circular Needles

Cast on the required number of stitches onto a circular needle. Slip half of the stitches to a second circular needle. Needle 1 holds the first group of stitches and needle 2 holds the rest of the stitches.

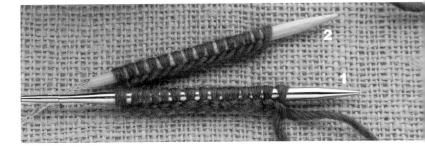

Step 1: Slide all stitches to other end of needles, making sure that needle 2 is on top, and needle 1 is on the bottom.

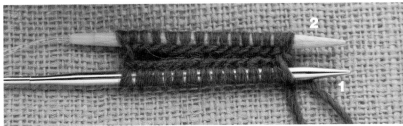

Step 2: Slip the first stitch from needle 1 and place onto needle 2. Slip the ending stitch from needle 2 up and over the stitch just transferred onto needle 1 to "join" into a ring.

Needle 1 Cable

Step 3: Pull needle 1 so the stitches rest on the cable.

Step 4: The working yarn is on needle 2, ready to work. Pick up the other end of needle 2 and work across all stitches.

Step 5: Turn the work so needle 1 is ready to work. Pull needle 2 so stitches rest on cable. Pick up opposite end of needle 1 and work across all stitches.

Continue in this manner until desired length is reached.

Short Rows

Short rows are partial rows of knitting, used to create curved sections of knitting. This is a particularly popular method for shaping heels and toes of socks. There are two basic techniques that are often used to close the gaps made by working short rows: wrap and turn, and working the wraps.

W&T (Wrap and Turn)

On the right side of work: Bring yarn to front of work between needles, slip the next stitch to the right-hand needle, move yarn to back of work to "wrap the stitch," slip the stitch back to left-hand needle, turn and purl back in other direction.

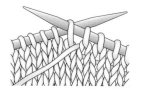
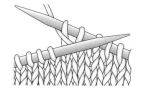

On the wrong side of work: Bring yarn to back of work between needles, slip next stitch to right-hand needle, move yarn to front of work to "wrap the stitch," slip the stitch back to the left-hand needle, turn and knit back in other direction.

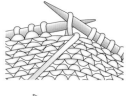

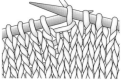

Working Wraps Together With Wrapped Stitches

On the right side of the work: Knit to wrapped stitch. Slip the next stitch from the left-hand needle to right-hand needle purlwise.

Use tip of left-hand needle to pick up wrap and place it on right-hand needle. Straighten the stitches out, move them back to the left-hand needle and knit the two stitches together.

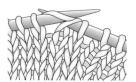

On the wrong side of the work: Purl to wrapped stitch. Slip the next stitch from the left-hand needle to the right-hand needle knitwise. Use tip of left-hand needle to pick up wrap and place it on right-hand needle.

Straighten out the stitches and move them back to left-hand needle and purl the two stitches together through the back loops.

Special note about working wraps: If you're working multiple wraps, there will be a single wrap on the first purl and knit rows. The following rows will have double wraps which will be worked by picking up two wraps instead of one, and then knitting or purling all three stitches together.

Crochet Provisional Cast-On

Step 1: With waste yarn, start by making a slip knot, and place the loop on a crochet hook.

Step 2: Make a crochet chain long enough to accommodate a few more than the desired number of stitches. Fasten off.

With the knitting needle, pick up one stitch in the back loop of each chain until you have the required number of cast on stitches. When you are ready to work the live stitches, simply unravel the waste yarn and place the stitches onto the knitting needle.

Yarn Resources

Berroco Inc.
1 Tupperware Dr. Suite 4
N. Smithfield, RI 02896-6815
(401) 769-1212
www.berroco.com

Louet North America
3425 Hands Road
Prescott, ON
Canada, K0E 1T0
(800) 897-6444
www.louet.com

Manos Del Uruguay
Wool Clasica Naturals
Distributed by:
Fairmount Fibers Ltd.
P.O. Box 2082
Philadelphia, PA 19103
(888) 566-9970
www.fairmountfibers.com

Plymouth Yarn Co.
500 Lafayette St.
Bristol, PA 19007
(215) 788-0459
www.plymouthyarn.com

Rowan Yarns
www.knitrowan.com

ShiBui Knits, LLC
1101 S.W. Alder St.
Portland, OR 97205
(503) 595-5898
www.shibuiknits.com

HOUSE of
WHITE
BIRCHES
PUBLISHERS
SINCE 1947

Simply Circular is published by DRG, 306 East Parr Road, Berne, IN 46711. Printed in USA. Copyright © 2011 DRG. All rights reserved. This publication may not be reproduced in part or in whole without written permission from the publisher.

RETAIL STORES: If you would like to carry this pattern book or any other DRG publications, visit DRGwholesale.com.

Every effort has been made to ensure that the instructions in this pattern book are complete and accurate. We cannot, however, take responsibility for human error, typographical mistakes or variations in individual work. Please visit AnniesCustomerCare.com to check for pattern updates.

ISBN: 978-1-59217-333-4
1 2 3 4 5 6 7 8 9

Photo Index

6

10

27

18

22

32

36

52

44

48